Isaiah

Isaiah

He saw Jesus' glory and spoke about Him

Copyright © Paul Blackham

The right of Paul Blackham to be identified as author of this work has been asserted by him in accordance with the Copyright, Designs and Patents Act 1988

First published 2011

All Rights Reserved. No part of this publication may be reproduced or transmitted in any form or by any means, electronic or mechanical including photocopying, recording, or any information storage and retrieval system, without permission in writing from the publisher.

Unless otherwise stated biblical quotations are taken from the Holy Bible, New International Version, Copyright © 1973, 1978, 1984 International Bible Society, used by permission of Zondervan Bible Publishers.

Scripture quotations marked (NLT) are taken from the Holy Bible, New Living Translation, Copyright © 1966. Used by permission of Tyndale House Publishers, Inc., Wheaton, Illinois 60189. All rights Reserved.

ISBN: 978-1-905975-34-1

Published by Biblical Frameworks

Reg. Office: 23 Coe Lane, Tarleton, Preston. PR4 6HH

Cover design, typesetting and production management by Verité CM Ltd, Worthing, West Sussex UK +44 (0) 1903 241975

Illustrations by Richard Thomas

Printed in England

Biblical Frameworks is registered in England No: 5712581
Charity No: 1116805.

Isaiah

Contents

Introductory thoughts from Paul Blackham 5

All about Book by Book 7

Introduction to Isaiah 9

Study 1 Human Shame 13

Study 2 Immanuel's Glory 23

Study 3 World Panorama 41

Study 4 Glory to the Righteous One 55

Study 5 The Glory of the Foundation Stone 67

Study 6 The Glory of the Angel of the LORD 83

Study 7 The Glory of the Servant 99

Study 8 The Glory of the Cross 115

Study 9 The Glory of the Gospel 129

Study 10 The Glory of the New Creation 143

Suggested Answers to the Bible Study Questions 157

Appendix 1 189

Appendix 2 191

The Statute of Liberty

Isaiah

I. Introductory thoughts from Paul Blackham

The longest chapter in the Bible is all about… the Bible! Psalm 119 is all about the wonder of the Word of God. Verse 103 shows us the heart of someone who really loved the Bible. He cries out to the LORD God:

Psalm 119:103 – "How sweet are your words to my taste, sweeter than honey to my mouth!"

Whether you are reading the Bible alone or in some kind of group with others, expect to be thrilled by the words of the Living God. This is not like reading any other book. When we read and study the Bible the ultimate Author can be present with you, showing you His words and applying them to you.

Thousands of small groups are starting up all over the world – but what is it that is going to sustain them? It has to be the Bible.

So often, people don't quite know what to do with these small groups. Meeting together, sharing testimonies and experiences or sharing the odd verse is ultimately too sparse a diet to sustain people's spiritual needs in the long run, and really help them to grow.

What is needed is confidence in the Bible, and the ability to go to a *book* of the Bible rather than just an isolated verse. Each book of the Bible was written with a purpose, and it is only as we digest it as a book that we understand the real message, purpose, direction, storyline and characters.

It's a lot easier than people often think. You might think, "Oh, I can't manage a whole book of the Bible", but what we're trying to do in Book by Book is to break it down and show that it's easy.

The Bible was written not for specialists, not for academics – it was written for the regular believers, down the ages.

The world is in desperate need for answers. How can the world live at peace? How can we live together with justice and truth and compassion? There are so many religions and so much division and bloodshed: what is the real and living way that takes us to the Living God who can give us all a new beginning?

The Bible is the answer of the Living God to all our questions.

Our desire is that many Christians would experience the joy and confidence in the Scriptures that is found throughout Psalm 119 – "How sweet are your words to my taste, sweeter than honey to my mouth!"

II. All about Book by Book

A. WHAT IS BOOK BY BOOK?

Book by Book is a Bible study resource with accompanying DVD. It has been designed principally for use in small groups, but can also be used for personal study or larger group situations.

B. THE STRUCTURE OF BOOK BY BOOK

The Study Guide

- A Key Truth to focus on the most important truth in that section of the Bible Book.
- A Mind-Map diagram giving an overview of the study.
- An explanation of the Bible text, divided under suitable headings.
- Further Questions to stimulate deeper thought and discussion.
- A week of suggested daily Bible readings to fill out and explore the themes from the study.
- A Bible Study with detailed questions, designed to lead the individual or group deeper into the text.
- A Bible Study answers section at the back of the study guide, for extra help if need be.

The DVD

Key features provided on each DVD are as follows:

- There is a 15 minute discussion on the DVD linked to each section of the Study Guide Bible passage
- The on-screen host is Richard Bewes, with co-host Paul Blackham. A specially invited guest joins them in the Bible discussions.

Isaiah

C. SOME TIPS ON HOW TO USE BOOK BY BOOK

The beauty of Book by Book is that it offers not only great Biblical depth, but also flexibility of approach to study. Whether you are preparing to lead a small group, or study alone you will find many options open to you.

And it doesn't matter if you are a new Christian or more experienced at leading Bible studies, Book by Book can be adapted to your situation. You don't need to be a specially trained leader.

Group study: preparing

- Select your study (preferably in the order of the book!)
- Watch the DVD programmes
- Read the commentary
- Use the suggested Bible Questions…
    …or formulate your own questions (the Mind Maps and Key Truths are a great guide for question structure).

Group study: suggested session structure

We recommend you set aside about an hour for each study:

- 5 minutes – read the relevant section of the Bible
- 15 minutes – Watch the DVD programme
- 30 minutes – work through the Bible Questions (either your own or the ones in the guide), allowing time for discussion
- 10 minutes – If the study got the group thinking about wider issues of life today, then consider the Further Questions to stimulate a broader discussion
- Taking it further – Suggest that group members look at some of the Daily Readings to follow up on the theme of the study

Given the volume of material you may even choose to take two weeks per study – using the DVD to generate discussion for one week and the Bible Questions for the next.

Individual study

There is no set way to conduct personal study – here are some ideas:

- Select your study (preferably in the order of the book!)
- Read the Bible passage and related commentary.
- Try looking at the Mind-Map diagrams and seeing how the book has a structure.
- Take a look at the Key Truths and decide if they are the same conclusions you had reached when you read the book.
- Perhaps focus on the week of daily Bible reading to help you to explore the rest of the Bible's teaching on the themes of each section of study.
- Work through the Bible Questions. Don't worry if you get stuck, there is an 'answers' section at the back of the guide!

Isaiah

III. An introduction to Isaiah

The whole earth is filled with the glory of Jesus and there can be no room for any of the shame, pride and sin of the human kingdoms or religions. The book of Isaiah shows us how the kingdoms of this world all fall under the judgment of Immanuel, the Anointed Servant, as He knocks down all that stands in His way as His Church goes out to all the peoples of the world.

Isaiah chapter 53 is quoted in the New Testament more than any other part of the Old Testament. Yet the whole book of Isaiah is referred to and quoted over and over again by Jesus and His apostles (See Appendix 1 for a comprehensive list of references). When they wanted to display the glory of Jesus (His mission and character), then Isaiah was of such great help. Long ago, hundreds of years before the human birth of Jesus of Nazareth, Isaiah met Jesus and saw His glory. As John says in John 12:41 – Isaiah "saw Jesus' glory and spoke about Him".[1]

That is the great theme of Isaiah's mighty book: the glory of Jesus. Isaiah challenges the Church and the world of his day (and every age) to turn away from the shame of the world, the flesh and the devil and turn to the revolutionary glory of Jesus, the Suffering Servant, Immanuel, the Mighty God, the Divine King. Though the fallen human world has "no soundness" yet Jesus is full of righteousness. Even though we are corrupt from head to toe (Isaiah 1:6), even though all human religion is worthless, even though the nations are full of idolatry and greed, yet the Living God has formed His own Church for a righteous eternal destiny through the glorious suffering work of Jesus. Both Jew and Gentile are joined together in the Church by the glorious Cross of Jesus, 'conquering' the world with His gospel.

The Holy Spirit had opened Isaiah's eyes to the worthless glory and shameful corruption of the human condition. Yet, the glory of the conquering King of Heaven, displayed most in His weakness and

---

[1] "Jesus our Jehovah – In Isaiah 6:5, when Isaiah saw his vision of heaven, with the Lord high and lifted up, he said, "Woe is me, for I am ruined! Because I am a man of unclean lips, And I live among a people of unclean lips; For my eyes have seen the King, the Lord (Jehovah) of hosts." Yet the apostle John, referring to this same incident, writes that Isaiah saw Christ's glory, "and he spoke of Him" (Jn. 12:41)… The simple fact is that Jehovah's Witnesses do not witness to the true Jehovah of Scripture. They reject His own witness and the witness of His Word that Christ Himself is Jehovah who came to earth in human flesh." (C. H. Spurgeon, sermon entitled *Who is Jehovah? Who is Jesus?*)

suffering, stands forever. The nations and the 'glory' of this passing age are decaying away, but the glory of Jesus grows on into that new creation future when even the lion and the lamb will live peacefully together.

We need to keep Deuteronomy 28 in mind as we read through Isaiah. The language of the blessings and curses of the Law come up time after time after time. Yet, Isaiah reminds us that the Law was looking at more than just the land of Canaan. The Law was always looking to that new creation future when Christ will renew the whole creation and pour out those blessings on the new heavens and the new earth.

This great book of Isaiah begins by telling us how many kings came and went while Isaiah was preaching: Uzziah, Jotham, Ahaz and Hezekiah. Isaiah saw these human kings come and go while he was preaching the gospel of Christ the LORD, the Everlasting King, perfect in righteousness and humble in service. Isaiah must have experienced all the hopes, fears and disturbance that each of these political orders brought, and he was appointed to preach about the Divine, Righteous King who was and is and always will be.

Approximate dates for the kings of Judah

King	Reigned from	Reigned until
Uzziah (Azariah)	790	739
Jotham (as co-regent)	750	739
Jotham in sole charge	739	731
Ahaz	735	715
Hezekiah	715	686

Isaiah's preaching work began the year that king Uzziah died (as we learn in chapter 6) around 739BC. Throughout more than 50 years Isaiah saw the terrible way that the nation of Judah tried to find security in religion or political alliances rather than in Christ the LORD. In the first five chapters Isaiah gives us a general picture of the society he lived in through his 50 years of preaching.

Uzziah was a good king who did what was right in the eyes of the LORD. He developed agricultural production (2 Chronicles 26:9-10); he defeated the Philistines and built new towns in their place (2 Chronicles 26:6-8);

Isaiah

and he built up the army to over 300,000 well-equipped soldiers with advanced military technology (2 Chronicles 26:11-15). However, in his pride he tried to offer incense in the temple as if he were an Aaronic priest and the LORD inflicted leprosy on him as he was trying to push through the protesting priests (2 Chronicles 26:16-23). He also failed to get rid of all the places of pagan worship (2 Kings 15:1-7).

Uzziah had leprosy for the rest of his life so he had to live apart from everyone else (2 Chronicles 26:21), and his son Jotham effectively managed the kingdom for him. After Uzziah died, when Jotham was 25 years old, he became king (2 Chronicles 27:1). Jotham also did what was right before the LORD but he did not root out the pagan practices in the country. Still there remained centres of pagan worship in the high places and the pagan shrines from Solomon's time were allowed to continue. Not until the reign of Josiah were all these evil places totally removed (2 Kings 23). Jotham managed to conquer the Ammonites and "grew powerful because he walked steadfastly before the LORD his God" (2 Chronicles 27:6).

However, when his son Ahaz became king, aged 20, he actually promoted pagan worship. He "made idols for worshipping the Baals. He burned sacrifices in the Valley of Ben Hinnom and sacrificed his children in the fire, engaging in the detestable practices of the nations" (2 Chronicles 28:2-4). So the LORD allowed the king of Israel to inflict heavy casualties on Judah (2 Chronicles 28:5-8), although Israel was unable to take Jerusalem (2 Kings 16:5). Ahaz tried to make an alliance with the king of Assyria, using the treasure from the temple, and when he met with the king of Assyria in Damascus he saw a pagan altar which he replicated in the temple of the LORD in Jerusalem (2 Kings 16:10-18).

Ahaz's son Hezekiah became king when he was 25 years old and he was faithful to the LORD God. He did his best to cleanse the temple of pagan influences (2 Chronicles 29; note also 31:1) and he led the whole of Israel and Judah in an incredible Passover celebration (2 Chronicles 30). While the temple was being consecrated so many animals were sacrificed that the ordinary Levites had to help the Aaronic priests with the preparation of the animals (2 Chronicles 29:32-35). In 2 Chronicles 31 the people of Judah started to celebrate all the different festivals, tithes and offerings that were originally described in the Law of Moses.

Though Hezekiah led these wonderful reforms, to what extent were the hearts of the people reformed as well? We see this concern throughout the book of Isaiah. These outward 'means of grace' are only pleasing to the LORD if they come from hearts that are full of love and trust towards Him. The rituals and offerings were only ever pointers towards the Person and Work of Jesus Christ the LORD and if He was ignored, if His glory was forgotten, then the 'Church activities' were meaningless.

Hezekiah looked to Christ the LORD for his security so when the armies of Assyria arrived, with great arrogance and blasphemy, the Angel of the LORD (one of the titles of Jesus in the Old Testament) went out and defeated the entire Assyrian army overnight (2 Chronicles 32:1-23).[2]

This is the great theme that Isaiah sets before us in his book. At the centre of reality is King Jesus in His great glory. He is the Servant King who lays down His life for His people, the conquering Messiah who in His resurrection redeems the whole creation to be the future home of righteousness forever and ever. Yet, our hearts and minds so easily put creatures of empty glory in His place: human power; money; religion and self-improvement. Isaiah thunders out against anything that takes the place of the glorious LORD Jesus, whether in the Church or in the societies outside. Jesus is for everybody, whether religious or not, whether Jew or Gentile, whether 'inside' or 'outside'.

---

2   The personal name of 'Jesus' occurs only rarely in the Old Testament and normally He is referred to simply as 'the LORD' or through some of the other Messiah-titles like 'Branch', 'Son', 'King', 'Angel of the LORD' etc. It is important for us to remember that God the Father has always sent God the Son as His mediator, in the power of the Spirit. It is very dangerous for us to think that in the Old Testament God the Father spoke for Himself without His Mediator but that in the New Testament He decided to have a Son to speak for Him instead! No, God the Son is and always has been the One Mediator between God and humanity. We see that in the creation of the universe itself when the Father created all things through the Son. We see the same thing all the way through the Hebrew Scriptures as Christ the LORD appears and speaks usually through the prophets. Perhaps the most basic Christian confession is that Jesus is the LORD. It is a wonderful thing when this ancient Mediator, God the Son, is born as one of us and pushes aside all the prophets and priests to speak simply and directly to everybody for Himself.

In this study guide, like all the other study guides in the Book by Book series, we will sometimes refer to Christ the LORD in the Old Testament using His name 'Jesus'. We do this for two reasons. First, the Church of the first and second century did this, including the apostles themselves as we see in Jude 5. It is only in relatively modern times that this practice has declined. Second, we normally refer to God the Son as 'Jesus' in all our songs and sermons, so it is good for us, especially for those new to the Bible, to make this strong connection to Him in the Old Testament just as in the New. When the New Testament writers refer to 'the Lord' most modern writers and preachers are happy to use the word 'Jesus' when they explain their meaning so perhaps it is helpful for us to sometimes do the same when the Old Testament writers refer to 'the Lord' as well.

Isaiah

Study 1   Human Shame: Isaiah 1:1–5:30

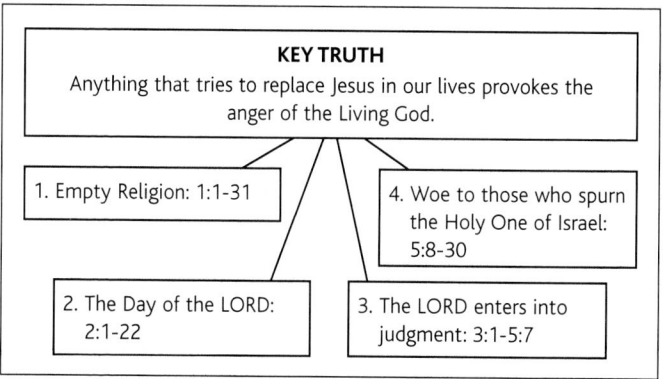

1. Empty Religion – 1:1-31

Sin is deeply unnatural. It seems impossible that the creatures of the Living God should turn against Him. All the plants and animals, the stars and angels, walk in step with His ways day after day, night after night. Yet, the human race has become so corrupt, so unnatural, that we instinctively turn away from the Living God. By nature we do what is evil and will not trust the One who made us. The book of Isaiah will expose the corruption, greed and foolish idolatry of all the nations around Israel, but from the beginning and all the way through, the greatest accusation is against the Church herself for the way she behaves towards her LORD.

Even the Church, the redeemed community that has been set free from that slavery of sin and condemnation, also turns against the LORD God. Even that community that was formed to show another way, the way of Life, often seems almost ignorant of her own LORD and Saviour!

Isaiah begins by calling on the whole creation to witness the bizarre and wicked behaviour of the Church: "Hear me, you heavens! Listen earth!" Even animals know who looks after them, but Israel does not have the understanding of an ox or donkey (verses 1-3).

To be lost in the darkness of paganism is one thing, but to actually forsake Jesus Christ, the Holy One of Israel, is the worst of all. When Christ the LORD is our life and strength, our peace and joy, then to turn our backs on Him is to hurt ourselves (verses 5-6). He alone can heal us. He alone can give us new birth and take away that deep corruption that covers every part of us.

The corruption inside Israel in Isaiah's day was reflected in the nation and countryside. Back in Deuteronomy 28-29, the LORD God established curses and blessings that would reflect the way His Church treated Him. If they loved and trusted Him, keeping all His commandments, then their life and environment would reflect that gracious friendship and love. However, if they turned against Him, spiritually committing adultery and refusing to love or trust Him, then the land would be under a curse. Isaiah begins by pointing out how the symptoms of this curse can already be seen in the land (verses 7-8).

Surely the worst cities in the whole Bible have to be Sodom and Gomorrah. Even in popular culture they are infamous for their immorality and ungodly living. Yet, Isaiah addresses the leaders of the nations as if they were the leaders of those cities – verse 10. It is only the grace of God that has prevented Jerusalem being judged just as Sodom and Gomorrah were – verse 9.

Yes, but surely Jerusalem isn't so bad! Jerusalem has the temple and sacrifices, festivals and prayer. How can such a 'religious' city be compared to those pagan places? Yet, in verses 11-15, the LORD cuts through all that religious pretence and hypocrisy. None of it means a thing unless it contains the true life of God from hearts that love Him and trust Him. He will not even listen to their prayers until they are right with Him (verse 15). He literally hates all these temple activities when the reality is not there. Hezekiah had re-established the new moon feasts (2 Chronicles 31:3) yet the LORD doesn't want them unless they are focussed on the Way of Christ.

In words that would later inspire James 1:26-27, the LORD describes the only kind of 'religion' that He will acknowledge – "Stop doing wrong, learn to do right! Seek justice, encourage the oppressed. Defend the cause of the fatherless, plead the cause of the widow" (verses 16-17).

Isaiah

After He was born through Mary, Jesus of Nazareth was the least 'religious' person in history and He was constantly in conflict with those who were hiding behind the ceremonies, rituals and outward appearance.

It is so unreasonable for us to pretend at religion and stay in the filth and corruption of our sins. If Israel would only stop and think clearly, then she could find cleansing and blessing from the LORD – verses 18-20. The curses of the Law could so easily become the blessings of the Law through repentance and faith.

The chapter concludes with two images: a city and an oak tree (verses 21-31). Just as 'The City' or London can represent the entire economic state of the United Kingdom or New York or Tokyo can stand for their nations, so Jerusalem, throughout the whole book, stands for the spiritual state of the nation. If she was once faithful, she is now more like a prostitute (verse 21). All her blessings have become cheap and nasty as she turns to greed, ignoring the widow and orphan (verses 22-23). She is like an addict who cannot heal herself and the LORD must intervene to bring about restoration (verses 24-28). He will reform the nation, getting rid of the sinners but preserving those who repent and trust in Christ. When the LORD Christ has saved His people then they will be righteous (verses 26-27).

Israel had been using 'sacred' oaks for their secret pagan worship, but like a dry old oak this must all be burnt up "with no-one to quench the fire" (verses 29-31).

Our secret sins – our love of money, entertainment, pride and 'religion' – cannot be hidden from the Holy One of Israel. The LORD Jesus sees all that we are doing and the true state of our hearts. If we will not turn to Him in repentance, love and trust, then we leave Him no alternative except to purge us and prune us through chastisement and suffering.

These opening chapters have no specific historical markers so they could apply to any and every year in Isaiah's ministry and challenge the Church in every age. It may be that Isaiah only began his preaching ministry after the commissioning of chapter 6 and he places these first chapters to give a sense of the circumstances he faced and the message he preached throughout his whole ministry.

2. The Day of the LORD – 2:1-22

If Israel had been absorbing the pagan practices of the surrounding nations, Isaiah set a much better vision before the Church of his day (2:1-5), a vision of the opposite influence, a time when people from all over the world would be followers of Christ the LORD.

> "The people intended by the Lord to be magnetic to the world (vv2-4) have, instead, allowed the world to magnetize them – into worldliness, fortune telling, attempts at collective security, acquisitiveness, militarism, false religion, humanism."[3]

If the *earthly* Jerusalem was an unfaithful prostitute, then the Jerusalem *above*, the mountain of the LORD, is exalted and glorious, full of the light of the LORD Himself. As Psalm 87 says, Gentiles from all over the world will be "born in Zion", fellow members of the LORD's family, united together in the Church, the heavenly city of God. Instead of being implacably opposed to one another, the nations find true peace and unity in the global, multinational Church of Christ the LORD. Perhaps verse 4 will not fully happen until the day of resurrection, but even now as we follow Jesus in loving our enemies and turning the other cheek we can begin to taste the future when the time of war will be ended – "They will beat their swords into ploughshares and their spears into pruning hooks" (2:4).

If we are going to deny ourselves now, in this passing age, we need to see the great hope and joy that is set before us. We can put the flesh to death only when we can see how it is all going to end. If we live with this glorious vision before us then we can begin to live that way even now, as the Church is a global, multinational community of peacemakers. Jesus has already been among us to teach us His ways (verse 3) so we can strain towards that resurrection future day by day where we work, in our neighbourhoods and in our families.

Yet, that great resurrection hope of Christ the LORD bringing universal peace to the whole world can only happen because on that Day He will first bring His great and terrible judgment against the world. The world can never be the everlasting home of righteousness until it has been

---

3   Alec Motyer in a letter from June 2011

Isaiah

cleansed of all the darkness, selfishness and evil that pollute it. Israel was full of false religion, superstition, greed and a deep confidence in human power (verses 6-9).

Therefore, they will not be able to stand on the Day of the LORD. When the glorious LORD Jesus comes in the "splendour of His majesty" people will try to hide in the caves (verse 10 and 19-21 – compare Revelation 6:15-17). In the light of Jesus' glory all human pride will be humbled (verse 11).

All the way through the book of Isaiah human and demonic pride is challenged. When the corrupt and selfish 'glory' of the creatures tries to replace or compete with the uncreated, self-sacrificial majestic glory of the LORD Jesus Christ, it provokes the deepest anger of the Living God. Notice how the Day of the LORD is all about destroying human pride and empty glory (verses 12-18).

Only the LORD Jesus Christ is worthy of our trust and love – "Stop trusting in human beings, who have but a breath in their nostrils. Why hold them in esteem?" (verse 22).

3. The LORD enters into judgment – 3:1-5:7

In our sin we place our confidence, our security, our comfort in anything other than the LORD Christ Himself. The Father has always sent Him to be our helper and our friend, our Saviour and our LORD, but we look to money, earthly leaders, sex, entertainment, houses, nationality, comfort or status to make us feel safe and secure.

So, when the LORD speaks of His judgment on Judah in chapter 3 He shows how He will take away all the created things that make them feel secure – whether food, water, "the hero and the warrior; the judge and the prophet; the diviner and the elder" – verses 2-3.

Again, through the book of Isaiah, we will see how the LORD God will shake up and cast down both the Church and the nations in order to break their grip on their false gods: the mere creatures that take the place of Jesus Christ.

The leaders of the nation, the ones who should care for the LORD's vineyard, have led His people astray – verses 12-15. False teaching always produces social injustice (verse 14-15) and sexual immorality (verses 16-17). If the men were taking pride in their military prowess, the women were obsessed with their appearance and their fashion (verses 18-26). Yet, when the LORD takes away their false security the men will have been killed off and the women will be deeply humiliated (4:1).

The colourful and striking imagery of Isaiah may disturb us or even shock us, but it arises from his passion for the glory of Jesus. How shameful it is when we choose the passing worthless treasures and strength of this life rather than the everlasting and glorious Word of Life, Jesus the Eternal Son!

The point of the judgment is not to bring shame on the men and women of Judah for its own sake. No! The LORD God takes away the false 'gods' only so that His people will cling to the true God, the Branch (4:2-6).

"The Branch" is a title for Christ, especially when He is considered as the King and Priest – (see Jeremiah 23:5; 33:15; Zechariah 3:8; 6:12). We are here thinking of a family tree and a Branch of the tree surviving and flourishing.

> "In 3:18 they sought a false, transient 'beauty' but now they discern true beauty in him and he beautifies them… 'Glory' had been their destruction (2:10) and 'pride' (2:12) their ruin. Now the divine glory dwells among them, they rightly pride themselves in him and he imparts a true dignity to them"[4]

The Messiah will deal with the sin and shame of Jerusalem – "He will cleanse the bloodstains from Jerusalem by the Spirit of judgment and the Spirit of fire" (4:4). Coming in the power of the Spirit, Jesus Christ would remove the sin and shame of His people by judgment and fire on the Cross. As we will see in such detail later in Isaiah, it is by the death of the LORD Jesus Christ that our sin is removed.

In the Exodus, after the judgment and salvation of the Passover, the Angel of the LORD (Jesus Christ Himself), travelled with the Church in the wilderness. He protected them and cared for them, defeating their enemies and giving daily bread from heaven and water from the rock. The pillar of cloud by day and fire by night constantly showed them that

---

4 Alec Motyer *The Prophecy of Isaiah*, IVP, 1999, page 54

Isaiah

He was with them. In the same way, when He has cleansed them through the Spirit of judgment and fire, He will be with them like that and they can take refuge in Him.

That wonderful vision of the Messiah from the Branch of David according to His human birth, but caring for them as He did long ago in the Exodus, is followed by the song of the vineyard. Isaiah's song describes how the LORD carefully planted His vineyard hoping for justice and righteousness (5:7), but instead finding only "bad fruit" (5:2). Even the people of Jerusalem and Judah must agree that anybody with such a useless vineyard would just destroy it. Having stated the problem of "bad fruit" the rest of chapter 5 goes into that accusation in much more detail.

4. Woe to those who spurn the Holy One of Israel – 5:8-30

This series of woes gets right to the heart of all the 'idols' that take the place of Jesus in our hearts.

Woe to those who think that property and beautiful homes will give security (5:8).

Woe to those who turn to alcohol to drown out their sorrows and silence the questions (5:11).

Woe to those who "are heroes at drinking wine and champions at mixing drinks" (5:22).

Woe to those who think that 'going out' and parties will make them happy (5:12)

In searching for life anywhere other than Jesus, there can be nothing but loneliness (5:8); barrenness (5:9-10); exile (5:13); hunger and thirst (5:13); death and hell (5:14); and humiliation (5:15).

Woe to those who are tired of waiting for the Living God to show His plans (5:19).

Woe to those "who call evil good and good evil, who put darkness for light and light for darkness" (5:20). It is so easy to convince ourselves that condemning sins of greed, lust, pride, gossip, vanity and laziness is just old-fashioned or merely the product of human cultures. Yet when we are so 'clever' that we no longer know what is good and evil we are in the depths of darkness and ignorance.

Woe to "those who are wise in their own eyes and clever in their own sight' (5:21). To be "wise in our own eyes" means that we think that we are so smart; that we have gained understanding through our own brain power; we judge our wisdom by our own vision rather than by the Wisdom of God.

Woe to those who allow injustice for greed (5:23).

All these ways of 'living' are so common in this dark age, and yet there is no life or substance in such an empty life. When the fires of judgment or the storms of life come, such a life is quickly destroyed (5:24). There is no future outside of Jesus, the Holy One of Israel.

The anger of the Living God is provoked against His vineyard and it is time for it to be destroyed (5:25-30). He has decided to call for the nations of the world to come to Jerusalem, not to worship there as in 2:1-5 but to carry out His judgment. Ready and eager for battle these nations come to leave Judah in chaos and darkness (5:30), as if Judah would be returned to the chaos and darkness of Genesis 1:2 before God the Word brought light, life and order.

Isaiah has presented us with a profound diagnosis of Judah and Jerusalem in his day. Though king Jotham tried to get rid of pagan practices, king Ahaz encouraged them. So, there may have been great excitement when Hezekiah did so much to destroy the pagan worship and restore true worship to the temple. However, what was going on in the hearts and minds of the ordinary people? Though they got involved in the Passover and offerings at the temple, yet they were still greedy, still getting drunk, still looking for security in their property, their appearance or their social life.

In these opening 5 chapters Isaiah forces the Church in every age to see that our lives and actions tell the truth about us, whether we really do love and follow Christ the LORD. We may pretend when we go to Church, but how do we really live day by day?

Is our Church life respectable on the surface but underneath it provokes the LORD God to judge us and chastise us?

Isaiah

Study 1 Bible Questions

Isaiah 2:1-22

1. Verse 2. Isaiah looks into the future, beyond the Jerusalem of his day at the new creation and the Mountain of the LORD (see Hebrews 12:22). Given the judgment on Jerusalem described in chapter 1, what was the purpose of this prophecy of 'the last days'?

2. Verses 2b-3. Think about the fears of the people of Jerusalem in terms of the armies and empires threatening them. How does the LORD's view of the world differ from theirs? How do these words still speak to us today?

3. Verse 4-5. Is this vision of a war-free world simply about our new creation future? What does it mean to live now with that hope in front of us? How does verse 5 relate to this?

4. Verses 6-8. The contrast with the state of Jerusalem in Isaiah's day is strong. List all the ways that the ancient Church had turned away from that new creation hope that Christ would bring.

5. Verse 9-12. It is as if Isaiah prays that the LORD will set everything right in verse 9. What is the final answer to this prayer?

6. Verses 13-18. How do all these images help us to understand what will happen on the Day of the LORD?

7. Verses 19-21. When the skies are filled with the glory of Christ the LORD, the arrogant world will try to flee underground. How does Isaiah show the revolution of that day?

8. Verse 22. This summary verse gives us one of the deep truths of the whole Bible. How do we feel this challenge in our own lives today?

Study 1 Further Questions

1. If the sinful corruption of humanity stretches to every part of us (see Isaiah 1:5-6), then how do we account for all the good and amazing things that human beings do, whether they are Christians or not?

2. Can religion ever be a good thing or does it always lead us away from the real and living LORD God? What about human traditions, buildings, rituals or festivals?

3. Isaiah 5:20 seems to speak powerfully to our age. Materialism and 'treasure on earth' is hardly noticed even within the Church family and in the wider world all kinds of evils are celebrated as good. Why have the values of the world invaded the Church so deeply?

Study 1 Daily Readings

Day 1	Isaiah 1:1-20
Day 2	Isaiah 1:21-2:5
Day 3	Isaiah 2:6-22
Day 4	Isaiah 3:1-26
Day 5	Isaiah 4:1-6
Day 6	Isaiah 5:1-7
Day 7	Isaiah 5:8-30

The daily Bible readings are an opportunity to not only read through all of the material in the book under study, but also to read parts of the Bible that relate to the themes and issues that we have been considering. Wetry to make sure that we receive light from the whole Bible as we think through the key issues each week.

Isaiah

Study 2 Immanuel's Glory: Isaiah 6:1-12:6

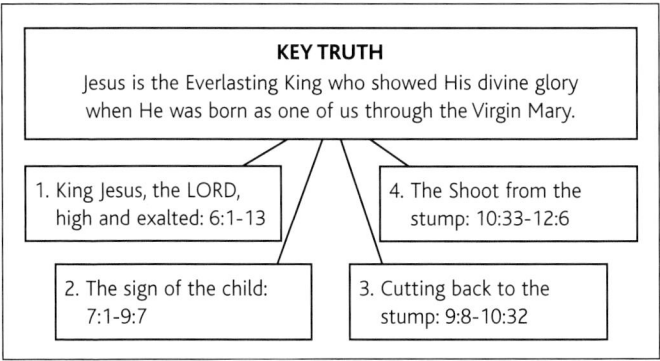

KEY TRUTH
Jesus is the Everlasting King who showed His divine glory when He was born as one of us through the Virgin Mary.

1. King Jesus, the LORD, high and exalted: 6:1-13
2. The sign of the child: 7:1-9:7
3. Cutting back to the stump: 9:8-10:32
4. The Shoot from the stump: 10:33-12:6

1. King Jesus, the LORD, high and exalted – 6:1-13

We are right back into the realm of specific history, at a specific time and place. Isaiah was in the temple in the centre of Jerusalem in the year that King Uzziah died. Uzziah had tried to get into that very temple to offer incense as if he were an Aaronic priest, and the LORD had struck him with leprosy as a punishment. He had spent his remaining years cut off from political life and unable to worship in the temple – according to the laws of Leviticus 14. Even in his death he had to be buried in a separate burial plot (2 Chronicles 26:23).[5] Jotham, his son, had already been acting as king in his place and now he was going to enthroned in an official sense. What would the future hold? Where could stability be found? Who could the ancient Church rely on if even a good king like Uzziah could fall so badly? Uzziah had reigned for 52 years, so perhaps Isaiah and the nation felt uncertain about the future when this great king was dying under the curse of leprosy.

---

5 "For years the king had lived in alienation and separation, under divine displeasure (2 Kings 15:5; 2 Chronicles 26:16ff), and as his death approached he remained, to the human eye, uncleansed. Thus, Uzziah, as the darkness of death closed in upon him, was symbolic of Isaiah's view of the nation, its plight and its problem." (Motyer, 75)

The true and everlasting King of heaven appeared to Isaiah in the temple.

> "He saw the Lord Jesus; so this vision is explained Jn. 12:41, that Isaiah now saw Christ's glory and spoke of him, which is an incontestable proof of the divinity of our Saviour. He it is who when, after his resurrection, he sat down on the right hand of God, did but sit down where he was before, Jn. 17:5" (Matthew Henry).

King Uzziah may have tried to force his way in, but King Jesus is so glorious, seated on His heavenly throne, that even the hem of His priestly robe filled the entire temple! (6:1). The temple itself was shaking in His presence.[6]

The earthly kings were served by earthly creatures that were corrupt and compromised, but this glorious and exalted King was attended by the wonderful seraphim (6:2-4). These amazing heavenly creatures are enthralled by and ever-fearful of the glory of the LORD Jesus.

Verse 3 is an extraordinary claim. Can the world really be full of His glory? As Isaiah had looked around at Judah and Jerusalem, not to mention the surrounding nations, he had seen endless sin and corruption. Yet, these burning angels declared that the whole earth is full of the glory of this Exalted King, the LORD Christ.[7]

We may sing "Jesus is LORD, creation's voice proclaims it", but do we really believe that His glory fills everything in His earth? Have we become so spiritually short-sighted and narrow-minded that we look at the world in a materialistic and atheistic way? Will we allow the Scriptures to correct our vision, showing us how to view the sun, moon, stars, mountains, sea, animals, our food and even ourselves as presentations of the glory of Jesus?

---

6   "Shaking is the customary reaction of earth to the divine presence" (Motyer, 77)

7   The Hebrew word seraphim literally means "burning ones" and given that the temple was filled with smoke (6:4), we must assume that there was plenty of fire around them (see Psalm 104:4). Each of the seraphs had 6 wings: two to fly with; two to cover their faces and two to cover their feet. As they flew around the temple, they constantly proclaimed the utter holiness of the LORD Almighty and the fact that the whole earth is full of His glory (6:3). Even these pure celestial creatures, who have never lived among the sin and corruption that we have done, dare not show their faces in the presence of the Holy One of Israel, the Glorious LORD Jesus. When they are in His immediate presence they are constantly shielding themselves from His majestic glory, using their wings for protective cover as a bird does while nesting. Yet, having experienced such exposure to the nature and personality of the Eternal Son, they declare that the whole earth is full of His manifested character, His glory.

Isaiah

In the presence of the glorious LORD Jesus, Isaiah is completely shaken, just as the temple itself was shaking. He may have lived a live of religious diligence coming to the temple, but when he is confronted by the real and living Messianic King, the Eternal Holy One of Israel, he knows how deeply sinful and corrupt he is. To see the King, the LORD Almighty, turns his world upside down (6:5). When the apostle John also saw Jesus in His glory, he too was completely shattered by the sight (Revelation 1:9-18). When we see Jesus "as He is" (1 John 3:2-3) we will become like Him.

In Isaiah chapter 5 it was all about woe to *other* people who have fallen into sin, but now Isaiah cries out "Woe to *me*! I am ruined". Not only are the people he lives with unclean but he is also a man of unclean lips (6:5). Isaiah's great gift was his speaking and writing. He is brilliant in his use of language and yet it is at that very point that he most feels his sin.[8]

The burning angels know what to do and one of them takes a coal from the altar and applies it to Isaiah's lips (6:6-7).

Sin can be the deliberate breaking of a known command or simply falling below the standard of perfection that is set for human life, the glory of God (Romans 3:23), and if the whole earth is full of His glory, then all our sin is constantly right before Him, right in the presence of His glory. If we also could see the glory of Jesus, the manifestation of who He really is, then we would feel just as Isaiah did.

The remedy for sin is atonement. Sin is not removed by mere repentance or sorrow. It can never be washed away by doing good work or beginning a 'fresh start in life'. Even in our own relationships we know that when we have deeply hurt someone, it is not good enough to cover it up with good behaviour or sweet words: the wrong needs to be properly confronted, exposed and dealt with.[9] If the sinless seraphim are so respectful of the divine holiness then our offences against this Holy and Majestic God clearly need a serious remedy. How can we put right what has gone wrong? If we have actually *angered* this exalted King by our actions,

---

8   The apostle Peter was a fisherman yet it was when the LORD Jesus gave him the miraculous catch of fish that Peter cried out "Go away from me, Lord; I am a sinful man!" (Luke 5:8). At our very strongest point is where we most keenly feel our sin.

9   In fact, if we refuse to face what we have done wrong then the 'sweet words' only create more offence and irritation.

words and even our thoughts and feelings, then how can we "make it up" to Him? What can we do or say or give that will soothe His anger and restore peace?

Right from Genesis 2:17 the consequence of our sin is death. If the earth is full of His glory then there is no place for any creature that defies or falls short of that glory. On the final day of judgment He will tell all who have sinned to depart from Him forever (Matthew 25:41). Yet, because He loves us so much He has shown a way for that death to be headed off, a way for the Divine anger to be soothed before that final judgment. As we will see in Isaiah 53, He died our death for us. He suffered the God-forsaken rejection that our sins require so that we can remain in His world, in His presence forever.

So, the seraph went to the altar of burnt offering where the fire was always kept burning. Here the sacrificial animals were daily presented to make atonement for sin, to act as a sign pointing forward to the future death of the Lamb of God, the Messiah Himself. Applying that coal to the lips of Isaiah was a painful, attention-grabbing reminder to him that the LORD had a way to take away His guilt and make atonement for him.

> The ever-burning fire of the altar stands for the ever burning hostility of holiness to sin. This fire of holiness is satisfied on a substitute offering. The 'live coal' symbolises the application to Isaiah of the satisfied fire of holiness. This is not 'purification by fire' but atonement by substitution.(Alec Motyer)

With atonement applied Isaiah is ready to hear the voice of the Divine King (6:8).

Who are the 'us' at the end of verse 8? It has been claimed that it is simply like Queen Victoria saying "*we* are not amused" whereby a monarch speaks in the plural. However, these words are referred to Jesus Himself in John 12:41 but also to the Holy Spirit in Acts 28:25-27. Therefore Christ is speaking on behalf of the whole Trinity when He requires a servant to preach for the Trinity here.

Isaiah is very willing to volunteer (6:8) but his mission is very discouraging: the effect of his gospel preaching would be to make people even harder, to close their ears to the truth (6:9-10). Whenever the good news of Jesus

Isaiah

Christ is preached it produces a reaction, either opening blind eyes or closing eyes more tightly; either bringing life or else bringing death. Whenever we are confronted with the Light of Christ we either come into His Light or else we retreat further into the darkness (John 3:19-21).[10]

Isaiah is given the task of preaching the truth with great clarity and power knowing that most people will not respond and instead become even more hardened in their selfishness and sin.[11]

Isaiah is alarmed at this prospect (6:11), but he is told that he must keep on with this mission until the exile comes (6:12), until everyone who has become blind and deaf has been taken away and the Holy Seed will remain as the stump in the land (6:13).

Verse 13 is very important. As we read through Isaiah we hear how the LORD's judgment is going to fall on Judah, on Israel, on all the surrounding nations, and finally on the whole heavens and the earth. It might be nice to imagine that there will always be a faithful few people who are good enough to survive the LORD's judgment, that we all have a chance if we are good enough, zealous enough, trusting enough. Yet, the truth is that none of us can stand on the Day of the LORD. In verse 13 it looks at first as if a tenth will remain, but then even that tenth is laid waste. In the end there is only One who remains: only One who can endure the Day of His Coming and that is Christ Himself. Isaiah will preach this same message to us over and over again throughout his book.

Jesus is the Glorious Holy One of Israel and everyone else must fall before Him.[12] Everybody is blind and deaf and even Isaiah is a man of unclean

---

10 See also Romans 1:21-32. When we turn from goodness and choose evil, our love for evil is strengthened and our hatred of the good is confirmed. We cannot reject Christ with impunity even right here and now, let alone the future day of judgment.

11 "Isaiah must preach to them, and they will hear him indeed, but that is all; they will not heed him; they will not understand him; they will not take any pains, nor use that application of mind which is necessary to the understanding of him; they are prejudiced against that which is the true intent and meaning of what he says, and therefore they will not understand him, or pretend they do not... Note, there are many who hear the sound of God's word, but do not feel the power of it... Forasmuch as they would not be made better by his ministry, they should be made worse by it; those that were wilfully blind should be judicially blinded (v. 10)." (Matthew Henry).

12 In Acts 3:14 Peter clearly states that Jesus is the Holy One of Israel.

lips. Jesus is the Holy Seed, the One to whom all the promises refer. He is the Seed of the Woman (Genesis 3:15); He is the Seed of Abraham (Genesis 12:7) and He is the Seed of David (2 Samuel 7:12). Jesus is the Holy Seed whose glory Isaiah saw.

2. The sign of the child – 7:1-9:7

From the glorious presence of Jesus we are right back into the turmoil of the kings of Judah (7:1). We skip over the reign of Jotham and arrive under the godless regime of Ahaz (7:1). Ahaz was so unfaithful to the LORD that he had actually sacrificed his own son in the fires to the pagan gods (2 Kings 16:3).[13] The Aramean king and the Israelite king formed an alliance to fight against Judah, presumably to force Judah into an alliance against the Assyrians. Although the military pressure was unsuccessful, Ahaz and his people were deeply shaken (verse 2) and were clearly thinking of forming an alliance of some kind with the Assyrians (which is what happened in 2 Kings 16:7-9).

Isaiah is a creative artist, full of visual imagery and powerful metaphors. Even in verse 2 he describes how the people were shaken "as the trees of the forest are shaken by the wind." All through the book we find a constant stream of intensifying metaphors and images. The LORD used these aspects of Isaiah in so many ways. For example, here in verse 3, we see that Isaiah had called his son "Shear-Jashub", meaning "a remnant will return".[14] So, as Isaiah was standing there delivering his message, his child was also standing there silently declaring, by his name, that judgment was coming but that a faithful remnant, a Faithful One, would be left over from the destructive fire.

If Ahaz is looking to human strength for his security, Isaiah is sent by the LORD to the place where presumably Ahaz was preparing water supplies for the anticipated siege of Jerusalem (7:3). The LORD tells Ahaz not to worry about Aram and Israel: they were both nations that were about to be wiped out within 65 years (7:8). The real issue is placed firmly before Ahaz – "if you do not stand firm in your faith, you will not stand at all" (7:9).

---

13 The irony must never escape us. The pagan gods demand so much from their followers, even the sacrifice of their children, yet the real and Living God sacrifices His own Son for our sake – a point that Isaiah makes abundantly clear.

14 Note that the surviving remnant is symbolised by just one man. In the end there is only One Man who survives the divine judgment on the world: Jesus Christ Himself.

Isaiah

Ahaz was a man lost in deep darkness, profoundly deaf and blind in the sense of 6:9-10. So, in a wonderful show of grace and mercy, the LORD offers Ahaz an incredible opportunity for a sign to prove the words of comfort that Isaiah had preached. Ahaz could ask for anything no matter how impossible. By way of comparison, his son Hezekiah would later ask that the shadow cast by the sun go back ten steps on his stairway (2 Kings 20:8-11; Isaiah 38:7–8; 2 Chronicles 32:24). The mind boggles at how difficult it might be to cause a shadow to do this. We may think of the miracle done for the Gibeonites in Joshua 10:12-14. Yet, Ahaz had no interest in proving the reality of the LORD God (7:12).[15]

Therefore the LORD God Himself sets out a sign that will prove His reality; a sign that would indicate His solution to all the troubles of His people; a sign that would show how the Church could stand firm in her faith in every generation. This was truly a sign beyond anything in "the deepest depths or in the highest heights". This prophecy of the birth of Jesus has become so precious to the Church of every age – "the virgin will conceive and give birth to a son and will call Him Immanuel" (7:14).[16] *Immanuel* means "God with us" and surely that is the greatest security for any and every crisis that we might face, whether an invading army or the crises of health and conflict in our own individual lives. By His virgin birth Jesus has become one of us.[17]

---

15 At first glance we might think that Ahaz is giving a godly answer if we compare it to the words of Jesus in Matthew 4:7. However, when we read the following words of Isaiah we realise that Ahaz simply has no interest in the LORD.

16 Some argue that the Hebrew word *alma* might only refer to a young woman rather than virgin. However, young women give birth to children every day all over the world and such an event is hardly a sign "in the deepest depths or in the highest heights"! *Bethulah* is the word for a young woman of marriageable age, married or unmarried, whereas *alma* is the Hebrew word for a virgin.

[17]

GLORY be to God on high, And peace on earth descend! God comes down, he bows the sky, And shows himself our friend: God the invisible appears! God, the blest, the great I AM, Sojourns in this vale of tears, And Jesus is his name.	Him the angels all adored, Their Maker and their King. Tidings of their humbled Lord They now to mortals bring. Emptied of his majesty, Of his dazzling glories shorn, Being's source begins to be, And God himself is born!	We, the sons of men, rejoice, The Prince of peace proclaim; With heaven's host lift up our voice, And shout Immanuel's name: Knees and hearts to him we bow; Of our flesh and of our bone, Jesus is our brother now, And God is all our own. (Charles Wesley 1707-1788)

By the time this Immanuel child was born the problem of king Rezin of Aram and king Remaliah of Israel would be long, long gone (7:15-16). If Ahaz would set his heart and mind on Christ then he would see things from such a bigger perspective and see how the house of David (verse 2) would not be utterly wiped out by any of these enemies. However, because of Ahaz's faithless sin a much bigger enemy than Aram or Israel was coming to destroy Judah: Assyria (7:17-25).[18]

If Isaiah already had a son who embodied the message (7:3) he is now told to father another son called "Speed to plunder; haste to spoils".[19] His name was to be publicly known and verified (8:2) before he was even born so that everyone would know about it. This son was planned to publicise the fact that the Assyrian armies would race in and sweep over Judah collecting their plunder with great speed — which is what the prophet describes in verses 6-10.

However, the Immanuel who would be born of the virgin in later generations was also already with His people even when the Assyrian armies would flood over the land (end of verse 8). Yes, even when His land and His people were suffering the punishment of their sin, yet He would be with them and bear it with them. Furthermore, the plans of Assyria to utterly destroy Judah would not be allowed to succeed precisely because Immanuel is with His people.

Grasping this identity between Jesus and His Church is vital to understand this whole section. The exalted LORD God whose glory filled the temple in chapter 6 is the same God who is with us as a newborn baby, born through the flesh and blood of an ordinary Hebrew woman (7:14). Even before this happened He already thought of Himself as completely one with His people, so that when they were persecuted He too is persecuted with them (cf Acts 9:4-5). When we read the

---

18 "The way of faith has been rejected. The king of Assyria has been adjudged a greater security than the Lord and his promises. What now follows has the inevitability of biblical logic: the alternatives to the way of salvation are always ways of destruction; those who hate wisdom love death (Proverbs 8:36)" (Motyer, 88).

19 It is fascinating to see that Isaiah was married to a prophetess (8:3). Some have suggested that this was an honorary title given to her because Isaiah was the great prophet, almost as if she was known as Mrs Prophet. However, it seems more likely that Isaiah married someone who shared his mission and passion in the service of the LORD Jesus.

Isaiah

extraordinary speech of the LORD that runs from verse 12 right down to the end of verse 18, we see that He speaks as if He were completely part of the people of Israel, seeing Himself as a member of the same family (verse 18).[20]

This incredible speech from the pre-incarnate LORD Jesus is introduced in such serious tones – "This is what the LORD says to me with His strong hand upon me…" So what does the LORD have to say?

Verses 12-13 are taken up by Peter in 1 Peter 3:14. If we are going to live as faithful followers of Jesus then our fear of the Living God must drive out all other fears. Ahaz was frightened of the invading armies but if he truly feared the LORD Almighty then he would have nothing else to fear.

Just as Moses called Christ the Rock (see Deuteronomy 32:4, 15-18, 30-31 and see also 1 Corinthians 10:4) so too Isaiah likes to refer to Christ as the Rock or Stone (8:14 and see also 28:16 and 1 Peter 2:4-8). Here the LORD refers to Himself as a Rock that can be a holy place or a refuge for them if they fear Him but if not then that Rock will make them stumble, fall and be broken (8:14-15).[21]

Verses 16-18 are extraordinary and worth careful meditation. The LORD Himself says that He "will wait for the LORD" and He will "put my trust in Him" (8:17). Hebrews 2:13 makes special mention of this. God the Son in His identification with His people joins them in waiting for and trusting in the LORD God. When Jesus became one of us, as Immanuel, born of a virgin, He fully entered into our experience and He Himself prayed and trusted, learned obedience and patience throughout His life. The Psalms take us deep into the personal prayer life of the LORD Jesus Christ as He put Isaiah 8:17 into practice. Consider for example Psalm 22 when He was on the Cross. Immanuel showed us how to wait for the LORD and

---

20 Note that in Hebrews 2:10-14 we are told how it was Jesus speaking the words of Isaiah 8:17-18 – " Both the one who makes men holy and those who are made holy are of the same family. So Jesus is not ashamed to call them brothers. He says… "I will put my trust in him." And again he says, "Here am I, and the children God has given me." Since the children have flesh and blood, he too shared in their humanity…"

21 "It is as if a rock were put across a road to block the traveller from danger but, in carelessness or scorn, he refuses the warning and stumbles to his death… The same God in his unchanging nature is both a sanctuary and snare; it depends on how people respond to his holiness." (Motyer, 95).

put our trust in Him in all the circumstances of life, including the times when the fear of death might threaten to overwhelm us.

The speaker of verse 18 is the same as verse 17, the Immanuel who suffers with His people and ensures that they will never be completely destroyed (8:8 and 10). Furthermore, the only child that has explicitly been called a sign is the virgin-born Immanuel of 7:14.[22]

Christ is happy to be associated with all those who trust Him and call them His own family.[23] Yes, Immanuel and His Church may be a rejected minority even in Judah, but they are still signs and symbols of Israel, the real Church of all ages, those who are born in Zion.[24]

Immanuel – God with us – was with His people in their current crisis and would be born of a virgin to actually become one of them. He was not ashamed to call them His family. They could turn to Him for strength and wisdom whenever they needed. Yet, instead they consulted mediums to try to contact the dead! (8:19-22). Instead of coming into the light of Immanuel, they were slipping into the darkness of death. Life was becoming meaningless and deeply depressing (8:22). Nothing satisfied them anymore (8:21) and instead of turning to God for help they were shaking their fists at Him in anger. The final destination of such a path would be the utter darkness of Hell (end of verse 22).

Yet, even for these people lost in darkness and for the Gentiles too lost in their own pagan darkness, all hope is not lost (9:1-2). Immanuel really would be born right among them, even in Galilee of the Gentiles, making the light shine in their lost darkness. The birth of Jesus would enlarge the nation (9:3) to even include all the Gentile nations, achieving a victory

---

22 At first glance it might be assumed that verse 18 is spoken by Isaiah as he volunteers himself once again (cf 6:8), together with his two specially named sons. Isaiah's name means "the LORD's salvation" and we have seen how his two sons Shear-Jashub(1) and Maher-Shalal-Hash-Baz(2) were also named to embody the prophetic message.
(1) "A remnant will return"
(2) "Speed to plunder; haste to the spoil"

23 John Gill, the 18th century Bible scholar, is right to explain this verse in terms of Jesus Christ – "Christ and his spiritual children: Christ the Immanuel, the son of the virgin, is "for a sign", given by the Lord himself, even of the same deliverance, Isaiah 7:14 and a sign of the love of God to his people, and of his care of them, and regard unto them."

24 Compare the reference to Zion here with Psalm 87. Jesus and His human family are all citizens of Zion, the heavenly Jerusalem, regardless of their circumstances or nationality on the earth.

Isaiah

over the Gentiles that war never could (9:3-5). All this will be possible because Immanuel will be born: "For to us a child is born, to us a son is given, and the government will be on His shoulders. And He will be called Wonderful Counsellor, Mighty God, Everlasting Father, Prince of Peace. Of the increase of His government and peace there will be no end. He will reign on David's throne and over His kingdom, establishing it and upholding it with justice and righteousness from that time on and for ever. The zeal of the LORD Almighty will accomplish this."

These world famous verses explain the birth, character and mission of the LORD Jesus Christ is such glorious terms. He is already God the Son, yet He is given to us. He not only suffers with His people, but He bears the leadership of the Church forever in a way that these earthly, sinful kings never could. Other kings conquer the world through war, but He will conquer the Gentiles through gospel evangelism and peace, bringing true justice and righteousness to the whole world.

Think of the four titles that this virgin-born Child will have: Wonderful Counsellor; Mighty God; Everlasting Father; Prince of Peace. Notice that this human child will be called *El Gibbor* (Mighty God), the very title given to the LORD (Yahweh) Himself in Isaiah 10:21.

In chapter 8:18 Christ the LORD spoke about His children in the Church family and so He is known as their "Everlasting Father". He is the father of the new human race; the Second Adam.

3. Cutting back to the stump – 9:8-10:32

Isaiah now turns from Judah and gives the same kind of message to Israel, with all its tribes and factions.[25]

That glorious hope of Christ, taking the Church from the land of Israel out to the whole world, is set in stark contrast to the arrogance, pride and shame of Israel. They believed that they could rebuild (9:10) a strong and

---

25 "The prophets regularly saw both of the divided kingdoms as within their sphere of ministry. Theologically the reason for this is that human sins and errors cannot thwart the purposes or rewrite the promises of God. The northern tribes had thrown off their Davidic allegiance (1 Kings 12:16) and apostasized from the Lord (1 Kings 12:25ff) but the Lord does not revise his plans in the light of this. All who are written unto life (4:3) will be brought home to Zion through the same Messianic policy and the same promised king." (Motyer, 106)

influential future with political alliances and pagan religion! However, that is not the future that the LORD wants for His people and instead He will strengthen her enemies – the Arameans and Philistines – and keep on with this judgment until they have been cut right down to size (9:14-15).

Notice the repeated sentence at the end of verses 12, 17, 21 and 10:4 – the LORD's anger is not satisfied with these judgments: there are more to come.

They should have returned to the LORD (9:13), but the leaders take them even further astray (9:16 and 10:1-3). This corruption affects everybody, from the top of society to the bottom (9:17). The wickedness of Israel destroys it and they even fight against each other (9:19-21).

Yes, Assyria would be used to bring about this judgment, but Assyria too will be judged for pride and arrogance (10:12-13). The Assyrians have their own agenda of destruction (10:7-11) rather than the LORD's concern for the Church and Immanuel. Assyria thinks that it has made itself strong and has built an empire through its own wisdom (10:13-14), but it is just like an axe, rod, saw or club, all needing someone to wield them. Every nation is just a tool in the hands of the Living God, and He alone decides what to do with them (10:15). Therefore, Assyria too will need to be cut back and humbled (10:16-19) by Christ, the Light of Israel.

The Immanuel who suffers with His people and calls them His family will also go out to avenge them and protect them.

> Isaiah "creates one of the Bible's central utterances about the relation between heaven and earth in human history… The thrust of the passage is clear: the absolute sovereignty of the Lord in the world. Without forester and carpenter, axe and saw lie lifeless… There is only one Agent and he does all things well. Under him, history is the outworking of moral providences. The Assyrian holocaust was not 'let loose' on the world; it was sent, directed where it was merited, kept within heaven's limits, and in the end Assyria was punished for its excesses." (Motyer, 113).

Just as the purging of Judah would lead to a new beginning in Christ the LORD, so the purging of Israel would clear away everyone and everything other than the Holy One of Israel. Israel will no longer trust in Assyria but

Isaiah

in Christ the LORD alone (verse 20). When He is standing alone as the only One who *can* stand on the day of judgment, then His people will return to Him and trust Him (10:20-23).

So, the Church does not need to fear the coming judgment from Assyria (10:24-34).[26] The judgment will not last long (verse 25) and then the LORD's judgment will be re-directed away from Israel and towards the Assyrians. He reminds them of how He cared for them in the Exodus and freed them from the Egyptians (10:26-27). Though they are taken into exile, the Church will be given an exodus from exile (note verses 26-27).

4. The Shoot from the stump – 10:33-12:6

Both Israel and Judah will be cut right back to the stump. The LORD will use Assyria to judge them and prune them, yet a faithful stump will be preserved.

Will there be many who are left, who are righteous and faithful to the LORD? No, in the end there is only One: Christ Himself.

Whether Isaiah examines Judah or any of the other nations of the world, there are none who are righteous, no not even one. Only Christ the LORD Himself is faithful. He is the Holy One of Israel.

It is important, as we go through Isaiah, to notice how often Christ is referred to as the Holy *ONE* of Israel. In all of Israel there is only one single Holy One: only one who can be left when the LORD's judgment has fallen on the world.[27]

Jesus Christ, the Branch (see 4:2-6) will be born from Jesse, a descendant of David, ready to be the Immanuel King who takes the government of God's kingdom.

Isaiah 11 is one of the greatest descriptions of the person and work of Jesus Christ in the whole Bible. Verse two gives us an incredible insight into His dependence on the Spirit for all that He does. As the name demands, the Messiah ("the Anointed One") will be full of the Spirit without measure (John 3:34).

---

26 Note that when the Hebrew Scriptures want to refer to the faithful saints of the Church they may be referred to as "in Zion" or even "born in Zion".

27 Notice that in Acts 3:14 Peter specifically says that Jesus is the Holy One, the Righteous One.

Often people think of the LORD Jesus almost as if He were an independent 'god' rather than a member of the Trinity. In other words, sometimes people forget that He is always sent from the Father in the power of the Spirit – in creation, revelation and redemption. Jesus Himself said that of Himself He could do nothing (John 5:30, see also Acts 10:38). It was the Puritan Thomas Goodwin who really opened my mind to the depths of these Spirit-prophecies of Isaiah. In Volume 6 of his works (*The Work of the Holy Ghost*), chapter 3, he outlines nine "of the works of the Holy Ghost upon Christ our Saviour":

The Holy Spirit:

1. Formed the human nature of Christ in the womb of Mary (Matthew 1:18).

2. Joined the divine and human natures (though Goodwin feels that this is properly ascribed to the Son more than the Father or Spirit – see Hebrews 2:16).

3. Consecrated Him to be the Christ, quoting Isaiah 11:2. "What is Messiah or Christos but the Most Holy One anointed? Daniel 9. Now, with what oil was Jesus anointed and so made Christ? Acts 10:38, 'God anointed Jesus of Nazareth with the Holy Ghost.' The Holy Ghost is that oil he is anointed with above his fellows; and he hath his name of Christ, which is the chief name of his person, from the Holy Ghost, as he hath that of Jesus for saving us, which is his work."

4. Consecrated Him to all His offices: prophet; priest and king (Luke 4:18).

5. Anointed Him with power to do all His miracles and all the good that He did (Acts 10:38; Matthew 12:28).

6. Raised Him from the dead (Romans 8:11).

7. Filled Him with glory at His ascension (Psalm 45).

8. Anointed Him as King in heaven (Acts 2:33-36).

9. Proclaims Him as King in human hearts (1 Corinthians 12:3; John 16:14).

Isaiah

Here, in Isaiah 11:2, we are especially shown how the Spirit gives Jesus wisdom, understanding, counsel, might, knowledge and delight in His proper fear of His LORD. This takes us so deep into the life of the Trinity! If one danger is to think of the Living God as just one person, then another danger might be to think of the Father, Son and Spirit as so distinct, so full of everything they need without each other, that we end up almost with the idea of three gods! However, in reality this One Living God is such a close communion of the Three, all wrapped up in the same life together, that they need each other for all they do. The Father does all His work through the Son, by sending Him to do His will and speak His word and the Spirit empowers the Son to do all that He does.

Everything that the Trinity does is from the Father, through the Son in the power of the Spirit.

Isaiah chapter 11 takes us from the birth of Immanuel right through to the day when He will judge the world and renew the whole creation. In verses 3-4 He will not make superficial judgments based on earthly values, but will get to the truth, making sure that the poor get a fair share of everything. The wicked will not be able to resist Him as He will destroy them with a word and a breath (see Revelation 19:15 and 21; 2 Thessalonians 2:8).

> "First, the Messiah buds forth and then, through him, new life for people becomes possible on a world-wide scale and the life of nature itself is transformed. Verses 6-8 offer three facets of the renewed creation and verse 9 is a concluding summary. First, in verse 6 there is the reconciliation of old hostilities, the allaying of old fears; predators (*wolf, leopard, lion*) and prey (*lamb, goat, calf, yearling*) are reconciled. So secure is this peace that a youngster can exercise the dominion originally given to humankind. Secondly, in verse 7 there is a change of nature within the beasts themselves: *cow* and *bear* eat the same food, as do *lion* and *ox*. There is also a change in the very order of things itself: the herbivoral nature of all the creatures points to Eden restored (Genesis 1:29-30). Thirdly, in verse 8 the curse removed. The enmity between the woman's seed and the serpent

is gone (Genesis 3:15)… Finally, in verse 9 the coming Eden is Mount Zion – a Zion which fills the whole earth. Peace (9a), holiness (9b) and 'knowing the LORD' (9c) pervades all." (Motyer, 124).

The Messiah is not only the Branch growing from the stump of Jesse (11:1) but He is also the Root of the stump! (11:10) He is the Root and the Shoot – the origin and the destination. He is older than His ancestors! What a wonderful and cryptic way of speaking of the glory of Christ the LORD!

Jesus Christ will summon His people from all the nations, raising up a banner for all the nations to rally to (11:10-16). Israel and Judah will be reconciled together (11:12-13) and the LORD's people will be able to return home from exile in Assyria just as they returned home from exile in Egypt in the Exodus (11:16).

Sheltering in that One Faithful Remnant, Christ Himself, the Church will survive the anger of the Living God (12:1-3). When the Church appreciates this then there will no longer be any confidence in political treaties or religious practices or pagan worship, because the LORD Himself, the Divine Messiah, "is my strength and my defence; He has become my salvation" (12:2). Only He can stand on the day of judgment and only He can provide safety for His people, both now and on that day.

In the book of Acts we see how Jesus did make 'Israel' or the Church a global nation, spreading out to all the nations. People from every nation can rally to the One Righteous person and join Israel, grafted in, whether Jew or Gentile. Isaiah chapter 12 is a celebration of this time of renewal and restoration when the LORD's anger is taken away. In 12:4-5 the great desire is that the Church will take this message out to the nations of the world – "let this be known to all the world."

If we are members of Zion, and if our trust really is in the Holy One of Israel, the LORD Jesus Christ, then not only must we be captivated by His glory but also thrilled to tell others about Him.

Isaiah

Study 2   Bible Questions

Isaiah 11:1-11

1. Verse 1. What is the meaning of the reference to Jesse? (see 1 Samuel 16:1). Why is it important to know that a shoot is coming from the stump of Jesse? (see 2 Samuel 7:12-13)

2. Verse 2. What does the word 'Messiah' (Hebrew) or 'Christ' (Greek) actually mean? Why is that relevant to the prophecy of verse 2?

3. We sometimes say that everything that God does is "from the Father, through the Son and in the power of the Spirit". How does this help us to appreciate verse 2?

4. Verse 3-4a. What is wrong with judging by what we see or hear? How do His judgments for the poor and needy show this?

5. Verse 4b. Why is important to know that Christ the LORD will ultimately strike the earth in judgment even though He first comes as the Suffering Servant?

6. Verses 6-8. For the animals to behave like this there would need to be far more than a superficial change to the world. Why does Isaiah pick these combinations of animals? How does this holistic vision of the animal world remind us of Eden at the beginning?

7. Verse 9. What is the fundamental explanation for the radically new biological order of the world?

8. Verses 10-11. What is the centrepiece and climax of the new creation? What is the goal of Christ's redemption?

Study 2   Further Questions

1. Why don't Church leaders have the kind of encounters with Christ and the angels today as Isaiah had in chapter 6?

2. In the 20th century several leading 'thinkers' suggested that the Virgin Birth of Jesus was not very important, that it made no real difference to who He is. What do we make of this idea? If we imagine that Jesus had been produced through a human father, would this make any difference to His holiness or divinity?

3. Isaiah gives us such real and specific descriptions of the new creation that Jesus will bring about. How seriously do we take his words about the lion and lamb lying down together? Do we have a truly 'physical' future hope?

Study 2   Daily Readings

Day 1	Isaiah 6:1-13
Day 2	Isaiah 7:1-25
Day 3	Isaiah 8:1-22
Day 4	Isaiah 9:1-21
Day 5	Isaiah 10:1-34
Day 6	Isaiah 11:1-16
Day 7	Isaiah 12:1-6

The daily Bible readings are an opportunity to not only read through all of the material in the book under study, but also to read parts of the Bible that relate to the themes and issues that we have been considering. Wetry to make sure that we receive light from the whole Bible as we think through the key issues each week.

Isaiah

Study 3 World Panorama: Isaiah 13:1-20:6

KEY TRUTH
The whole earth is filled with the glory of Jesus and there can be no room for any of the shame, pride and sin of the human kingdoms or religions.

1. Babylon and its king: 13:1-14:27
2. Humbling the neighbours: 14:28-17:14
3. The African empires: 18:1-20:6

1. Babylon and its king – 13:1-14:27

When we live in the shadow of mighty empires of this world, whether they are religious or political regimes or multi-national companies or even the control of family or work in our own circumstances, we need to remember that none of them are going to last. Everything that can be shaken is going to be shaken, torn down and destroyed (see Hebrews 12:26-28). The empires and tyrannies, with all the injustice and suffering, of this passing age will be wiped away when the LORD Jesus Christ returns to the world in great glory to renew the whole creation and make the kingdoms of this world into His kingdom (Revelation 11:15). Even now He brings down the arrogant empires and systems that stand in the way of His plans for the Church.

> "The most striking use of the city motif is 'the tale of two cities'. The ongoing history of the world produces a global society structured without God, the humanly-made, humanly-centred city, created by human cleverness for human salvation... With the inevitable divine overthrow of this city there is created the 'city of God', a new world order constructed by God on his plan, with himself at the centre and from where he reigns over a universe of righteousness and peace." (Motyer, 17).

The prophecy that deals with Babylon and the spiritual powers behind her is split into three parts:

- the judgment of the world (13:1-16);
- the judgment of Babylon (13:17-14:2 and 20b-27);
- the judgment of Babylon's king, both human and demonic (14:3-20).

Ancient Mesopotamia (modern Iraq) was divided into two competing states: Assyria and Babylon. Assyria was the ruling power, but the Babylonians were on the way up. Isaiah looks beyond the rise of Babylon to its future fall, yet the subject of 'Babylon' has a wider and deeper context than the immediate time of Isaiah.

At the centre of a developing empire was the city of Babylon. It may have had its origins in the building of the tower of Babel described in Genesis 11:1-9, and the name Babylon seems to mean something like "Gate of the gods", indicating the pagan religion associated with that city from its earliest times. Throughout the Bible Babylon has a symbolic value, indicating the whole of this world's order in its opposition to the Living God. The reason that Revelation chapters 17 and 18 are all about Babylon is because those chapters are really about the overthrow of this world's order of greed, power and injustice. This section of Isaiah takes such a big and cosmic perspective because the fall of Babylon is really the fall of the kingdoms of this world.[28]

So, if the banner was raised to summon the nations into the Church in 11:12, now the banner is raised to gather the holy ones for war: the final war of global destruction when the Rider on the White Horse rides out against the whole world — see Revelation 19:11-21. Verses 1-5 introduce the coming judgment for Babylon, but then from verses 6-13 we are shown the global judgment that the Messiah will bring to the whole creation, the heavens and the earth.

---

28 Revelation 17.5; 18:1-3. "the more we think of chapters 13-27 as a study of the principles of world history merging forward into eschatology, the easier it becomes to see that from the start Babylon carries overtones of the 'city of emptiness' (24:10) whose fall is the end of all that opposes the Lord's rule" (Motyer, 142).

Isaiah

> "Because the LORD has set his hand to a moral judgment that is cosmic (verse 10) and world-wide (verse 11) in extent *the heavens tremble* and *the earth will shake*. The ordered movement of the heavens and the stability of the earth, all that was achieved by creation, will be undone in judgment." (Motyer, 139).

Having rejected the Glorious Immanuel who cares for His flock, the world is like "sheep without a shepherd" (verse 14). Though they run to find a place of safety, there is nowhere to hide and even the women and children suffer the destruction.

Having convinced us that all the nations of the world, even the sun, moon and stars, will be shaken down on the LORD's day of judgment, in 13:17 the camera zooms down to the much nearer target of Babylon itself in the time of Isaiah.[29]

The Medes and the Persians brought about the destruction of Babylon in 539BC, as Isaiah prophesied here (13:17) more than 150 years before it happened! The kind of total judgment that will happen at the very end on that final Day of the LORD's anger will fall on Babylon much sooner, just as it did on Sodom and Gomorrah (verse 19). There is no future for the Babylonian kingdom.

However, the judgment on Babylon (and the world) is only the other side of the one great covenant plan (14:1-2). The Church does have a future, and that future involves all the nations of the world (verse 2). Through the gospel of Jesus Christ, Israel has gone out across the world 'conquering' the nations, bringing them into the global family of the Church – "they will make captives of their captors and rule over their oppressors."![30]

---

[29] "The day of the Lord has many interim fulfillments. 14:17-22 will find one such in the overthrow of Assyria. Further on in history, it will be foreshadowed again in the fall of Babylon… In this way verses 17-22 are related to verses 2-16. It is not that Isaiah is here naming retrospectively the warriors who were summoned in verses 2-5; that summoning awaits the day, which even in our time, is yet to come. But the same principles that operate in that climactic day of history operate throughout. The God whom that day reveals is the God who directs history now, and sinful human nature, which will then be seen in its true colours, is the nature which drives people on today." (Motyer, 140)

[30] "The reality of all this is the spreading kingdom of peace into which the convert presses gladly and by choice and takes the servant's place within the community of grace." (Motyer, 142)

In the King James Version of the Bible Isaiah 14:12 is translated as "How art thou fallen from heaven, O Lucifer, son of the morning." The name *Lucifer* is taken from the Latin translation of the Hebrew Scriptures meaning "bearer of light", but it occurs only in this one place. It is not clear that Isaiah is primarily referring to the fall of the devil here. The prophecy as a whole seems to refer to the human ruler of Babylon in a highly symbolic judgment, but it is quite possible that Isaiah is also speaking about the devil in the background.[31] Certainly the words of 14:12-15 are very appropriate both to the attitude of the devil but also his fate as cast down to the earth, crawling on his belly and finally doomed to hell itself.[32]

The tyrant of Babylon is doomed to fall and his reign is spoken of as if it has already ended. The tyranny over the other nations will be broken and then the people can rejoice (14:5-8). When this king is killed, Sheol, the realm of the dead (sometimes represented as '*hell*'), is stirred up because the punishment of death has even reached this one that seemed untouchable (14:9-11). As his body rots, so he is brought down to the same level as everybody else. He acted as if he were a god, as if he could reach up to the highest heaven itself, yet he ends up at the very bottom of creation with all the rubbish, awaiting the final judgment of Hell itself.[33] This king will be humiliated in death (14:16-20).

The wicked will not be resurrected to inherit the earth (verse 21), but rather they are simply to be forgotten. Babylon, with all that she represents and any of the demonic forces that control her, have no place in Jesus' renewed creation – "I will sweep her with the broom of destruction, declares the LORD Almighty" (verse 23).

---

31 In Ezekiel 28 we find two remarkable prophecies: one to the "ruler of Tyre", a man who thinks he is a god; and then another prophecy to the "king of Tyre", a guardian cherub who was in Eden who fell into sin and had to be thrown out. Perhaps here too Isaiah is speaking of the ruler in the heavenly realms, the prince of Babylon, the power behind the throne of this great symbolic city of worldliness, greed and corruption (cf. Daniel 10:13). If the glorious LORD Jesus is the Messiah-King behind the city of Zion in the heavens, then Satan himself is the ruler of the city of man, the city of the world and the flesh.

32 Verse 12 may be referring to two of the astrological gods of the Babylonian pantheon or even specifically to the plant Venus, also known as the morning star, which can be seen 'falling down' even as the sun rises.

33 Note: Sheol or Hades is the place that the wicked go when they die to await the general resurrection and the final judgment of Hell itself. The righteous are delivered from Sheol and wait with the LORD Jesus Himself in paradise (see Psalm 86:13).

Isaiah

All that Isaiah has spoken in this long prophecy of judgment is fixed, planned and determined by the LORD Almighty (14:25-27). The whole earth is filled with the glory of Jesus and there can be no room for any of the shame, pride and sin of the human kingdoms or religions.

2. Humbling the neighbours – 14:28-17:14

Having painted the big picture of judgment on the whole world and the specific judgment on Babylon as the symbolic centre of the human world in rebellion against the Living God, the words of judgment now come much closer to home, to the peoples immediately surrounding Judah. The Assyrians were still dominant and seeking to expand to the west. Egypt was another great power to the south, themselves being pushed by the Cushite empire to their south. How could the smaller states of Syria based in Damascus, Philistia, Moab, Judah and Israel survive among the rise and fall of these great powers? Could they or even should they join together in an alliance? Should they try to negotiate treaties with Egypt or Assyria in order to buy some security?

Over the next 20 chapters the prophet Isaiah addresses these deep questions, not by explaining clever political strategies but by pronouncing the LORD's judgment on every security other than Christ the Rock.

These nations may try to find a glory of their own or look to the glories of each other, but to reject the glory of the LORD Jesus is to invite judgment.

The Philistines (14:28-32)

In the year that Ahaz died, the Philistines receive this word of judgment (verse 28). Ahaz had been embroiled in power politics, having been defeated by the Arameans from Damascus (2 Chronicles 28:5) and suffering heavy casualties from the Israelites (2 Chronicles 28:5-8). Ahaz had paid the Assyrians (using treasures from the temple) to fight back against the Edomites and the Philistines (2 Chronicles 28:16-21, see also 2 Kings 16:5-9).

Perhaps the Philistines were rejoicing that Ahaz was dead and his Assyrian allies had failed (verse 28). However, Isaiah warns them that the new king (a viper) will bring destruction to them, as Hezekiah does in 2 Kings 18:5-8. He takes back the towns they had captured and defeats them in their own land (14:29-31). Even those who survive the battle die through famine (verse 30). The Philistines may be rejoicing at the thought of Judah's fall, but Immanuel has established His people and will never let them fall.

The Philistines may have no refuge in their coming conflict, but for those who look to Him the LORD has established Zion as a refuge for all His afflicted people (verse 32). Is this an offer for the Philistine people to find refuge in Zion, in Christ Himself, even as their judgment comes upon them?

The Moabites (15:1-16:14)

The structure of these two chapters is important to keep in mind. Throughout the prophecies of judgment the LORD weeps over Moab and at the centre of the prophecy is a description of the Moabites being offered a way to join the people of God in Zion under the peaceful reign of Christ Himself (the son of David).

- 15:1-9 – The judgment and humiliation of Moab.
- 16:1-5 – Moabites offered refuge in Zion through trusting in the Promised Messiah.
- 16:6-14 – Further judgment on Moab's pride (16:6) and paganism (16:12).

The tribes of Jacob had a strange relationship with the Moabites, the descendants of Lot. In one sense they were 'relatives', both looking back to men who had trusted in Christ (even though Lot had not been the best example of living out that faith!), but they were also drawn into conflict at different times.[34] However, in this long prophecy it is made clear that "the promises which will be fulfilled for David in Zion are for all who will take refuge there" even if they are Moabites.[35]

---

[34] The reference to Zoar in 15:5 is perhaps a subtle way of reminding the Moabites of their shameful origins, described in Genesis 19:30-38.

[35] See Motyer, 149.

Isaiah

Chapter 15 begins as if we are in the aftermath of the sudden destruction of Moab (15:1). Everywhere we look people are humiliated and mourning (verses 2-3), with grief and despair in every city. Verse 5 begins with a the LORD God Himself weeping over and with Moab yet promising to bring "still more upon Dimon" (verse 9). All through Isaiah we see the glory of the LORD Jesus as He not only judges the world who forsakes Him but also goes out to them with genuine compassion, offering them life and security if they will find their refuge in Him.

Chapter 16 takes us to a different scene with refugees arriving in Zion, bringing lambs for sacrifice, asking for shelter. Then in 16:4-5 Isaiah describes how Christ the LORD will bring peace to the world (cf. 2:3-5; 9:5; 11:6-9) – "One who in judging seeks justice and speeds the cause of righteousness" (16:5).

Moab needed to take this offer of refuge in Christ to heart and make a speedy decision to seek Him because within three years (16:14) the judgment was going to fall. The glory of Moab would be swept away, but the glory of Jesus remains as a refuge for her. We all imagine that life will go on just as it has, yet for us all, and for the whole world, the day of judgment is coming. We cannot postpone it or pause its advance for even one second. There is refuge in Christ Jesus, secured by His death and resurrection, yet the time is short.[36]

Jesus words in Luke 21:33-36 could have been spoken to Moab, and to us all – "Heaven and earth will pass away, but my words will never pass away. Be careful, or your hearts will be weighed down with dissipation, drunkenness and the anxieties of life, and that day will close on you unexpectedly like a trap. For it will come upon all those who live on the face of the whole earth. Be always on the watch, and pray that you may be able to escape all that is about to happen, and that you may be able to stand before the Son of Man."

---

[36] "In their location after verses 1-5, verses 6-13 warn Moab that there can be no 'cheap grace' in recourse to Zion and David. They have to face the falsity of their pride (v.6), the reality of their suffering (vv 7-11), the failure of their religion (v12), and the prospect that the future will be even worse than the past (vv 13-14). Then they need to return to their confession in verses 1-5 and make it a description of their future." (Goldingay – New International Biblical Commentary, Isaiah, Hendrickson 2001, page 111)

Damascus (17:1-14)

The same pattern is used against Damascus, a sandwich of judgments with a gospel filling.

- 17:1-5 – The judgment of Damascus (representing the kingdom of Aram) and the removal of its glory.
- 17:6-8 – Looking to the Rock, their Saviour, the Holy One of Israel.
- 17:9-14 – The judgment for forgetting Christ the Rock.

Notice how Aram and Ephraim are treated as an alliance here, which presumably reflects the politics of the day as the northern kingdom of Israel joined with others for security. Aram will suffer this fading and wasting (verses 3-4) to bring them down to a realisation of their true state. The glory of Israel, Judah and Damascus must fade so that only the glory of Jesus Christ remains.[37] When the false glory that draws the Arameans away from Christ is removed, then they can "turn their eyes to the Holy One of Israel" (verse 7). The idolatry will have been cleansed away (verse 8). Whenever the LORD is called the Rock (verse 10) we are reminded of the words of the apostle Paul in 1 Corinthians 10:4 – "that Rock was Christ". The judgments will take away all the Aramean security.

The nations are like the chaotic restless sea (verse 12) instead of taking refuge in the solid, immovable Rock of Christ.

3. The African empires – 18:1-20:6

The empire of Cush seems to be an empire to the south of Egypt, and it has a very distinguished role in the Bible. It is first mentioned in Genesis 2:13 when one of the great Edenic rivers flows out to Cush, presumably the original ancestor of the river Nile as we know it today. Later Cush is identified as one of Noah's grandchildren, a child of Ham, who himself was the father of Nimrod (Genesis 10:8; see also 1 Chronicles 1:8). The empire of Xerxes in Esther 1:1 stretches all the way from India in the east and Cush in the west. The Ethiopian empire of Cush sometimes took control of her north African neighbour Egypt, but they are distinct empires with

---

37 Again, the end of verse 3 sounds as if a remnant of Damascus will survive the judgment and it will be like the remaining glory of Israel. But then we are told that this glory must fade and waste away. Just as the tenth will also be laid waste in 6:13, so the remnant also must fade and waste away here. Only Christ, the Holy One of Israel, can remain. In verse 6 he states that the judgment will be so complete that only two or three survive, but then in verse 7 in turns out that there is in fact only one Holy One in Israel.

Isaiah

separate histories. Both Psalms 68 and 87 speak about people from Cush and Egypt coming to join Israel, finding their true identity as citizens of Zion. So, as we read these prophecies about Cush and Egypt we need to see how these nations have long been involved in the Biblical story.

Cush – (18:1-7)

Cush is introduced as a land of flying insects, great rivers (cf Genesis 2:13), papyrus boats and tall, impressive, smooth-skinned people. They send out ambassadors to make political alliances (verse 2). Yet, the LORD is not impressed with the security offered by Cush or her arrogance among the nations. As Cush tries to expand her influence and empire, the LORD will cut her back to size (verse 5). Notice the extent of the pruning in verses 6-7. All is cut down and left out for the animals. When the grapes are getting ready to mature, then all the branches are cut off with no harvest left at all. Is there then no hope for Cush? Not in Cush itself, but the people of Cush will come to Zion to trust in the Name of the LORD Almighty (verse 7). In Zion Christ is the One who remains even after all the judgments and pruning have been done.

Over and over again, the same pattern that was established in Judah is played out in all the nations. The LORD wants to bring people to Himself from every nation, all across the world. He comes in judgment to destroy them so that the wicked can be cut away and burned up, so that Christ Himself is left as the only place of refuge.

Egypt – (19:1-25)

In Exodus the Angel of the LORD[38], Christ Himself, came on the night of the Passover bringing judgment so He comes again to Egypt, causing deep fear (19:1). They will turn against each other and their worship of the dead (with their mummies) will come to nothing (verse 2-3) as they are conquered. The Nile is the great life source of Egypt, and that too will fail them (verses 5-10). The Egyptian wise men will become like drunkards, unable to make any sense (verses 11-15). If other nations were used to judge Judah, He is ready to use Judah to bring judgment on the Egyptians (verses 16-17).

---

38 To see how the LORD Himself, the Angel of God, brought judgment to Egypt and deliverance to His people see also Exodus 11:4-8; 12:27; 13:18-22 and 14:19-24.

Yet, again this judgment is designed to make Egypt forsake its religion of death and turn to the LORD Christ. We don't know which five cities are the focus of verse 18, but they will have become followers of the LORD Almighty. Just as Abraham, Isaac and Jacob built altars and monuments to the LORD God in the book of Genesis, so the Egyptians will have the same history for themselves (verse 19). When Israel was in slavery in Egypt, they cried out and the Angel of the LORD came down to rescue them (see Exodus 3:1-6). So, now the same 'exodus' will be given to the Egyptians if they too cry out to Him – "He will send them a Saviour and Defender, and He will rescue them." When the Israelites were rescued they were taught how to make offerings and sacrifices at Mount Sinai, so the Egyptians will be taught to make the same offerings (verse 21). This time His plagues on Egypt will be to heal them, to rescue them from their own pagan tyranny (verse 22).

In a glorious conclusion Assyria joins in the worship of Christ the LORD with Israel and Egypt. A glorious highway running from Baghdad to Cairo, via Jerusalem, stretches right across the Promised Land as it was originally defined to Abraham in Genesis 15:18-21. All three are defined equally as the LORD's people, His Church – "Blessed be Egypt my people; Assyria my handiwork, and Israel my inheritance" (verse 25).

> "They shall have an interest in the great Redeemer… Doubtless Jesus Christ is the Saviour and the great one here spoken of, whom God will send the glad tidings of to the Egyptians, and by whom he will deliver them out of the hands of their enemies, that they may serve him without fear, Luke i. 74, 75. Jesus Christ delivered the Gentile nations from the service of dumb idols, and did himself both purchase and preach liberty to the captives… They shall come into the communion of saints. Being joined to the Lord, they shall be added to the Church, and be incorporated with all the saints." (Matthew Henry).[39]

---

39 "The knowledge of God shall prevail among them, v. 21. They shall have the means of knowledge. For many ages in Judah only was God known, for there only were the lively oracles found; but now the Lord, and his name and will, shall be known to Egypt. Perhaps this may in part refer to the translation of the Old Testament out of Hebrew into Greek by the LXX., which was done at Alexandria in Egypt, by the command of Ptolemy king of Egypt; and it was the first time that the scriptures were translated into any other language. By the help of this (the Grecian monarchy having introduced their language into that country) the Lord was known to Egypt, and a happy omen and means it was of his being further known." (Matthew Henry).

Isaiah

Egypt and Cush – (20:1-6)

However, there is a further warning to Egypt and Cush. The Philistines put their trust in an alliance with Egypt, but Sargon of Assyria came to Ashdod and defeated them (20:1). To vividly and disturbingly proclaim the foolishness of trusting in Egypt or Cush the LORD told Isaiah to remove all his clothes for three years (verse 3) as a constant sign in Jerusalem of the way the Egyptians and Cushites would be taken away to exile in shame. "Those who trusted in Cush and boasted in Egypt will be dismayed and put to shame."

Isaiah confronts us with his powerful words and images, but in living naked for three years he must have created a scandal around the Jerusalem temple. This shocking way of vividly presenting the message was necessary because the profound question of trusting in Egypt was going to be the top issue facing Judah over the coming years.

We so often pretend to be civilised and respectable when in reality we are full of darkness and unbelief. If the Living God has to offend our sensibilities to get our attention then so be it. If He needs to destroy all our comforts and securities before we will look to Him for refuge, then so be it. Our hard and narrow hearts will rarely listen to simple reason, as Isaiah was told in 6:9-10.

We might complain of feeling embarrassed about sharing the message of Jesus with our friends, neighbours or colleagues at work. Yet, if Jesus asked us to live like Isaiah for three years, are we so passionate for Jesus that we would obey? It is unlikely that He would ask such behaviour of us, but what of the simple teaching that He has given to us all. Do we follow that with the same total abandonment and passion that we see in Isaiah?

Would we be fools for Christ if it meant that people might be won for Him?

Study 3   Bible Questions

Isaiah 17:1-14

1. Verses 1-3. Damascus was the capital of the kingdom of Aram, yet the LORD announced a judgment of destruction against it such that flocks of sheep will be free to graze right where the mighty city once stood. Why did the Arameans (and us still today) need to know that no matter how impressive our cities might be, they have no future?

2. Verse 4. Why does Isaiah make us think of Jacob as a large man who has wasted away with age and illness?

3. Verses 5-6. Another image shows us the corn field and the olive orchard after the harvest has finished. What is the power of this image? Is there any hope at all?

4. Verse 7-8. What is the purpose behind this cutting down of human pride? Who is our Maker and who is 'the Holy One of Israel'? Is the fundamental character of an idol that it is "the work of (our) hands"?

5. Verse 9. Imagine the city or town where we live being deserted and overgrown with weeds. How does this change our perspective on the life or 'glory' of that town or city?

6. Verses 10-11. The apostle Paul reminds us that the Rock of Israel was Christ Himself (1 Corinthians 10:4). What happened when those ancient people forgot Him?

7. Verses 12-13. How does Isaiah present the rising arrogance and pride of the nations? What is the response of the Rock to this raging sea?

8. Verse 14. Sudden disaster can take any or all of us away. What is Isaiah's message as we face such an uncertain future?

Isaiah

Study 3 Further Questions

1. More than one thinker has suggested that cities are one of the main problems in the world and that it would be better for us all to live in a much more 'spread out' way in the countryside. On the other hand at the centre of the new creation is the vast City of God, the home of the Father Himself. What are the strengths and weaknesses of cities, where humanity is all gathered tightly together?

2. If the LORD God humbled nations in the past through war, economic decline and diseases, then do we believe that He still does that to nations today? Can we see any evidence of this in recent history?

Study 3 Daily Readings

Day 1	Isaiah 13:1-22
Day 2	Isaiah 14:1-32
Day 3	Isaiah 15:1-16:14
Day 4	Isaiah 17:1-14
Day 5	Isaiah 18:1-7
Day 6	Isaiah 19:1-15
Day 7	Isaiah 19:16-20:6

The daily Bible readings are an opportunity to not only read through all of the material in the book under study, but also to read parts of the Bible that relate to the themes and issues that we have been considering. We try to make sure that we receive light from the whole Bible as we think through the key issues each week.

Seven brides for one brother

Isaiah

Study 4 Glory to the Righteous One: Isaiah 21:1-27:13

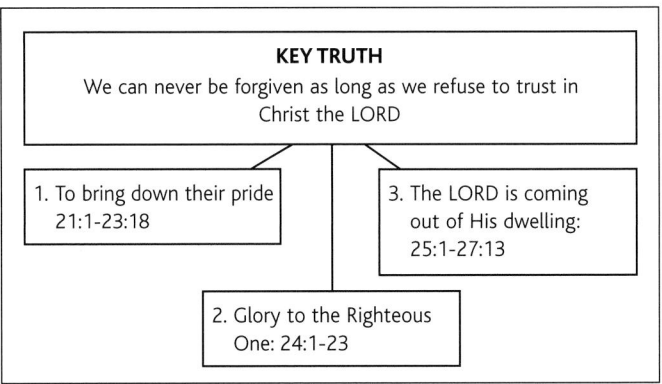

1. To bring down their pride – 21:1-23:18

The new cycle of prophecies goes back to Babylon to begin again. Babylon is the symbolic city of this world. The judgment and fall of Babylon means the judgment and fall of all cities and nations. This chapter of Isaiah is the key background reference for John's visions about the global fall of Babylon in Revelation 17-18. From this new vision of global judgment, Isaiah once again announces coming darkness and judgment for the nations around Judah.

The whole earth is filled with the glory of Jesus and there can be no room for any of the shame, pride and sin of the human kingdoms or religions.

The gods are fallen (21:1-10)

The great threat during this time in history was not from Babylon but Assyria. Babylon may have been trying to promote uprisings against the great Assyrian empire but it would be 100 years before the golden age of Babylon under Nebuchadnezzar. So, as this prophecy begins we might at first think that it is about the fall of Assyria, yet only in verse 9 do we see that it is about the fall of Babylon. This most likely refers to Sennacherib's destruction of Babylon in 689BC, towards the end of Hezekiah's reign.[40]

The Elamites and the Medes were laying siege (verse 2) and Isaiah is overwhelmed by what he sees (verses 3-4). Yet, Isaiah seems to be watching from Jerusalem and he is trying to rouse the city (verse 5) to take note of what is happening. The destruction of Babylon was an urgent warning about the destruction that was coming to Jerusalem very soon. A watchman is posted to look for news of what is happening (verses 6-9) and finally a man in a chariot brings the news: "Babylon has fallen, has fallen! All the images of its gods lie shattered on the ground" (verse 9).

In Revelation 14:8, as the three angels announce the divine judgment on the whole world, they quote Isaiah 21:9. Babylon, with its greed, luxury and worship of false gods, represents the world in its opposition to the Living God. If Babylon falls under the LORD's judgment then all who are with her must also fall under judgment, as Revelation 14 makes so clear.

This is wonderful news for the Church who is crushed and attacked by the world in every generation. The gods of this world will all be cast down in judgment and destruction. Now they may all seem so powerful, but none of them have any lasting future. Babylon will fall. This glorious announcement must comfort us too as we see the religious, political and financial empires of our age with all their tyrannical arrogance, persecuting the Bride of Christ. There is only room for one woman in the world filled with Christ's glory – and it is not Babylon (see Revelation 17:1-6 and 19:7-9).

> "The cryptic title (1a) indicates that Isaiah is looking beyond a historical incident to the Babylon which first appeared in Shinar (Genesis 11:1ff) and encapsulated in the spirit of self-sufficiency, the confidence of human beings that they could find security through their own technological expertise. It is that Babylon he has in mind as he warns the people of God to maintain their separate identity (cf. 52:11)." (Motyer, 176).

---

40 "Sennacherib records that he filled the city with corpses, 'the gods dwelling therein – the hands of my people took them and… smashed them.' The buildings and walls were razed and, says Erlandsson, 'his final gesture was to have huge volumes of water released over the ruins… to obliterate every trace of that city which had been constantly in revolt.'" (Motyer, 172)

Isaiah

Edom and Arabia (21:11-17)

Looking towards the south, Judah's nearest neighbours were the Edomites and the Arabs. For Edom there is darkness, and the great question is "how long will this darkness last?" The fearful news is that although the morning will eventually come, yet so will the night, over and over again.

> "As history moves forward, greater darkness envelops the world, bringing greater uncertainty – 'where is everything going?'... Thus a solitary Gentile experience mirrors world history: the end will come, the end is not yet. Hope lies in the undated future and though it is deferred it is sure." (Motyer, 177).

War and refugees are coming into Arabia as well (verses 13-15), to these other members of Abraham's family. Kedar was the first son of Ishmael, Abraham's son (Genesis 25:13). The strength of these desert bowmen will be gone, even within one year of this prophecy. Why? Because the LORD, the God of Israel, has spoken. In Isaiah 42 we will see how these Abrahamites are among the very first to welcome the Messiah, so this time of judgment and "cutting back to the stump" of Christ alone will also bring salvation among the Ishmaelites.

The Valley of Vision (22:1-25)

Three prophecies are brought together in chapter 22: Jerusalem (verses 1-14); Shebna (verses 15-19) and Eliakim (verses 20-25). Their common theme is the sin of trusting in this world and its resources rather than the glorious LORD Jesus.

How can the *mountain* of Jerusalem be a *valley* of vision? Perhaps Isaiah is showing how the sin of the people has turned everything upside down. For Isaiah the mountain has become a valley (see verse 4), a place of sin and darkness, a place where the city is destroying itself without any invading armies harming them (verses 2-3). Yes, the streets may be full of parties (verse 2), but if they could see the judgment that is coming there would be only deep sorrow. The armies of judgment are gathering (verses 6-7) and the LORD has taken away His protection from Judah (verse 8).

2 Kings 20:20 and 2 Chronicles 32:30 describe how Hezekiah organised a major engineering feat of providing water into the city. Yet, in verses 9-

11 Isaiah is not impressed. This made the people even more trusting of their own strength and technology rather than trusting in Christ who alone could give them true security. He can give them Living Water from the ancient waters of life (verse 11), but they did not look to Him.

Verses 12-13 provide the stark contrast. The people are living a high life of celebration and security (verses 13) when the LORD Almighty is summoning them to a time of deep repentance and weeping. They were putting on their best party clothes when they needed to put on their sackcloth. They were spending time on hairdressing when they needed to tear out their hair (verse 12) in profound sorrow.

The sin that cannot ever be forgiven is that of ignoring the LORD Himself. All other sins can be atoned for and forgiven when we look to Christ the LORD for forgiveness, but if we refuse to look to Him then we can never find forgiveness for any of our sins. Verse 14 states this judgment in blunt and direct terms. If we do not look to the Rock, to the Atoning Sacrifice, to Jesus Himself, then as long as we live we will never find atonement for our sin.

Shebna,(verses 15-19) was building fortifications in Jerusalem and taking pride in the Judean chariots (verse 18), yet his pride would be turned to disgrace when he was removed from his position. He would be replaced by the LORD's servant Eliakim (verses 20-25), a man who would offer much better leadership for Jerusalem and Judah. He would handle the legacy of David properly (verse 22-23). However, his family would try to load him up with their own glory and therefore he too would eventually be knocked down to size (verse 25).

Whenever anyone tries to rival the glory of Christ the LORD they must be humbled and removed.

Tyre and Sidon (23:1-18)

Tyre was the powerful trading base for a mighty mercantile empire spread right across the Mediterranean Sea, as far as Tarshish in Spain. Cyprus (verse 1), Egypt (verses 3-5) and Sidon were all dependent on Tyre's trading empire and would be completely stunned if it was ever destroyed. Yet the glory of Tyre must also be humbled so that even the business obsessed Tyre might also be involved in what the LORD is doing (verse 18).

"The LORD Almighty planned it, to bring down her pride in all her splendour and to humble all who are renowned on the earth" (verse 9). This same principle comes up over and over again throughout Isaiah. The whole earth is filled with the glory of Jesus and there can be no room for any of the shame, pride and sin of the human kingdoms or religions.

2. Glory to the Righteous One – 24:1-23

In chapters 24-27 of Isaiah there is a sequence of praise or rejoicing after each of the major prophecies of judgment.

- The *judgment* of the whole earth (24:1-13)
- The song of *praise* – Glory to Jesus! (24:14-16)
- The *judgment* of the heavens and the earth (24:17-23)
- The song of new creation *praise* (25:1-9)
- The *judgment* of Moab, bringing down their pride (25:10-12)
- The song of *praise* – trusting in the Rock (26:1-19)
- The day of *judgment* on the devil (26:20-27:13)

Isaiah has shown us the same pattern over and over again. The LORD God will not ignore or forget the nations of the world. He claims them all for His own and He will not give them over to darkness and sin. He will come in judgment on all the nations to destroy their 'glory', showing them that there is only the Glory of Christ the LORD. He alone can stand the fire of the LORD's presence. Christ alone can be the refuge for all the nations of the world.

Yes, the judgments are terrible but these judgments reveal how there is no lasting security or glory in any of military plans, alliances or fortifications. There is no security in any mere creatures.

Only Christ the Rock can be the true refuge and strength for anybody and everybody in every circumstance.

Chapter 24 takes this to the whole earth. A day is coming when not just each of the individual nations, one by one, but the whole earth on a global scale must be judged and destroyed (24:1). This will affect everybody regardless of their status or occupation (verse 2 cf. Revelation 19:17-18). The earth itself has become defiled by the wickedness of humanity and is withering away (verses 4-6). The civilisations of this passing order must be destroyed so Christ the LORD remains to renew the whole earth as the everlasting home of righteousness.

Notice again the pattern of judgment-gospel-judgment. In verses 14-16, between the two descriptions of the earth's judgment and destruction, comes the earth's singing, from east and west, "Glory to the Righteous One". That faithful remnant from the whole earth will acknowledge the glory of Jesus when all the false glory of corrupt humanity has been taken away. Even the glory of the sun and moon will fade away before the uncreated glory of Jesus (verse 23).

3. The LORD is coming out of His dwelling – 25:1-27:13

Chapter 25 is mostly a song of praise that we will sing in that new creation future when the earth has been shattered but made again, when we live in the glory of the resurrection with Jesus, the Father and the Spirit forever and ever. On that day, while the wicked are judged the humble saints will find refuge in the LORD. Then the marriage supper of the Lamb will be for all peoples (verse 6). Death itself will be destroyed (verse 7 – cf 1 Corinthians 15:54-55) and the LORD will personally wipe away "the tears from all faces" (verse 8 – cf Revelation 21:4). In the sheer joy of that day we will realise that we are there simply because we trusted Jesus (verse 9) and not by any wisdom or power or glory of our own.

This chapter is full of our new creation future in such vivid and clear terms. Until death is destroyed our tears can never be fully wiped away.

Yet, we must always remember that the new creation is only possible in the aftermath of the day of judgment. Until the world has been cleansed from all the sin and darkness it can never be the everlasting home of righteousness. So, after the first song of praise we are taken back into a prophecy of judgment. Moab is selected in verses 10-12 as symbolic of all the wicked. Just as Satan is crushed under Christ's feet, so the wicked are trodden underfoot on that day (verse 10). They will be thrown into a lake not of fire but of manure and their pride will be brought right down low, "to the ground, to the very dust" (verses 11-12).

Isaiah

All the time throughout Isaiah the challenge to the glory of Jesus will be brought down, in various historical acts of judgment here and now but in that final day of judgment on a global and cosmic scale. The glory of Jesus is that He provides safety and refuge for all those who trust in Him, both now and forever.

Chapter 26 takes us back into a song of praise. The righteous have a city with foundations, whose builder and maker is the Living God Himself (verses 1-2 – cf Hebrews 11:10 and 16). Jesus is the eternal Rock in whom we trust (verses 3-4 cf 1Corinthians 10:4). When we read Isaiah's prophecies we might feel as if history is an endless turmoil of war and destruction, of judgment and danger. Yet, those who trust in Christ find "perfect peace" and calm through it all (verse 3). Again, the proud and the ones who have raised themselves too high must be brought down and put under the feet of the poor and oppressed (verses 5-6).

When the righteous trust in the Righteous One they find that their way through life is level and smooth. Through all the hardships and suffering, we find His presence with us and we know where we are going and how to live each day. The key to this wisdom of the righteous is that instead of looking out for themselves they look to the LORD Jesus Christ and say "your name and renown are the desire of our hearts" (verse 8). Day or night, we long for Him and His people learn how to be more like Him. Yet, the wicked do not learn from Him whether He is kind to them or punishes them (verses 10-11). They do not acknowledge His glory (end of verse 10).

The righteous recognise that any honour that they have, anything they have ever done of any value, *"you have done for us"* (verse 12). Though we might have a boss at work and all kinds of earthly authorities have power over us, yet "your name alone do we honour" (verse 13). The wicked, who tried to make a name for themselves, have been judged by the LORD and they have no future. There will be no resurrection life for them (verse 14) and they are simply forgotten. Their glory is for *this* life only.

In all that the LORD Jesus does for the Church He has gained glory for Himself (verse 15). In His creation, revelation and redemption, His life, death, resurrection and ascension, He has revealed who He is: the Servant

King, the Dying Conqueror, the Sacrificial Priest. We are joyful to acknowledge that we could not save ourselves. We were in pain, as if we were pregnant, yet all that we produced was wind as if we had digestive problems (verses 16-18). But, in contrast, the LORD Jesus is totally fruitful in His painful labours: His dead will be resurrected to eternal glory with Him (verse 19). The spirits of the dead that belong to Jesus are refreshed by Him.

So, in the day of judgment, we can take shelter as He comes from heaven to destroy the wicked. The LORD is coming out of His dwelling in the heavens (verse 21) to punish the earth for all its sins. How can the Church survive such a global and comprehensive judgment? We shelter under the sign of His blood and therefore His anger will pass over us (verse 20-21 cf the Passover in Exodus 11-13).

That final day of judgment will finally deal with the devil himself (27:1).[41] If He is coming from His dwelling to sort out the whole world, then His "fierce, great and powerful sword" will be used to destroy the devil:

"I saw heaven standing open and there before me was a white horse, whose rider is called Faithful and True. With justice he judges and makes war... Out of his mouth comes a sharp sword with which to strike down the nations. "He will rule them with an iron sceptre." He treads the winepress of the fury of the wrath of God Almighty... The rest of them were killed with the sword that came out of the mouth of the rider on the horse..." (Revelation 19:11-21).

> "Notice how the triple description of the Lord's sword as fierce, great and powerful matches the triple description of his foes (*serpent... serpent... monster*)... The picture of the power of the air, the coiling serpent on the ground and the 'dragon which is in the sea' shows the whole creation infested with alien powers which will be sought and destroyed wherever they are" (Motyer, 222).

---

41 In order to appreciate the identity of Leviathan, note how the book of Job begins with Satan coming in to cause trouble in the courts of heaven and then the whole book reaches that climactic chapter 41 when the greatest power of the LORD is shown in His ability to defeat and tame Leviathan.

Isaiah

The LORD Jesus wields His sword so protectively because He is watching over His vineyard. Day and night He guards it (27:3). The choice for His enemies is clear: destruction or surrender (27:4-5). He would prefer His enemies to come to Him to make peace, but if they will not then it means battle and fire. His vineyard will have fruit all over the world (verse 6) so now He must bring His judgment down to show how there is no hope in anyone other than Himself. Even His own vineyard is filled with people "without understanding" (verse 11).

This time of judgment will reach right across the Promised Land of Genesis 15:18-21, from Egypt to Assyria (verses 12-13). When the trumpet finally sounds, there will be people from all over the world who have trusted in Christ alone and they will be gathered back together from all these nations.[42]

---

42 See Zechariah 9:14; Matthew 24:31; 1 Corinthians 15:52; 1 Thessalonians 4:16. "...there will be Gentiles awaiting the great trumpet heralding their full atonement... From the ends of the earth, and even from the supreme oppressors themselves (Egypt the first, Assyria the contemporary), there will be those whom the atonement trumpet calls to Zion. The gathered Gentiles will worship the LORD on the holy mountain in Jerusalem. They will be united to the Lord in worship, full participants in the holy community and welcomed in Jerusalem as members of the strong city itself (cf Ephesians 3:6)." (Motyer, 226)

Study 4 Bible Questions

Isaiah 26:1-13

1. Verse 1. In chapter 24 Isaiah confronted us with the destruction of the whole earth under the LORD's judgment. Even the powers in the heavens will be judged (24:21). The cities of this age will all crumble away (25:2). However, what enduring hope does the Church have in every age?

2. Verse 2. What is the entry requirement to enter into this strong and eternal city of God?

3. Verse 3. How can we have peace even when everything in our lives seems to be falling apart?

4. Verse 4. How does Isaiah encourage us to trust in Christ the eternal Rock?

5. Verses 5-6. What is the alternative to trusting Him? What is the outcome of that?

6. Verses 7-8. We might worry that the road ahead of us is completely broken and full of holes, but how can we walk on a level and smooth road through life? What must capture our hearts even when fears and pain surround us?

7. Verses 9-11. Describe the difference between the righteous and the wicked. Can we say they have different hearts and different eyes?

8. Verse 12. How are we to think of the fruit we produce in life?

9. Verse 13. How are we to cope with the forces and empires that try to control us? What can we do if even the government opposes us? How can we support our brothers and sisters who are in constant danger from oppressive regimes?

Isaiah

Study 4 Further Questions

1. Given that all the nations of the world are passing away and their glory is judged by the Living God, how should the Christians deal with issues of patriotism and nationalism? How important should our nationality be to us? When the glory of our nations is brought into that new creation future, how different will our nations seem then? (see Revelation 21:26)

2. How can we keep a balance between our hope of heaven when we die and our hope of the new creation on the final day when Christ the LORD returns? If we think only of the final hope we can lose the personal comfort of "absent from the body, present with the Lord", but on the other hand if we think only of going to be with Him in heaven we lose sight of the grand and holistic regeneration of all things that is the goal of salvation.

Study 4 Daily Readings

Day 1	Isaiah 21:1-17
Day 2	Isaiah 22:1-25
Day 3	Isaiah 23:1-18
Day 4	Isaiah 24:1-23
Day 5	Isaiah 25:1-12
Day 6	Isaiah 26:1-21
Day 7	Isaiah 27:1-13

The daily Bible readings are an opportunity to not only read through all of the material in the book under study, but also to read parts of the Bible that relate to the themes and issues that we have been considering. Wetry to make sure that we receive light from the whole Bible as we think through the key issues each week.

In the land of the blind

Isaiah

Study 5 The Glory of the Foundation Stone: Isaiah 28:1-35:10

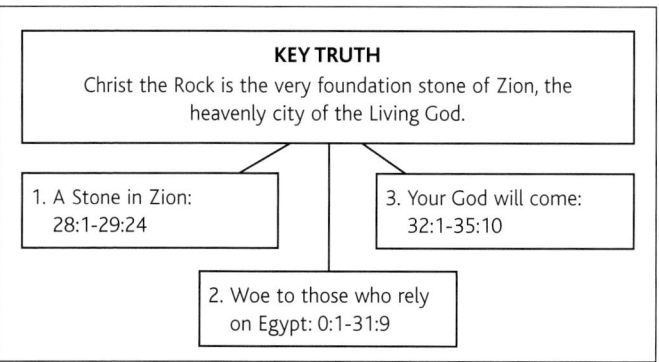

KEY TRUTH
Christ the Rock is the very foundation stone of Zion, the heavenly city of the Living God.

1. A Stone in Zion: 28:1-29:24

2. Woe to those who rely on Egypt: 0:1-31:9

3. Your God will come: 32:1-35:10

In the most complete manuscript of Isaiah from the Dead Sea Scrolls the book of Isaiah is divided into two halves after chapter 33. It is as if the book has two distinct parts, the first dealing with Isaiah as an ambassador of the LORD Jesus to Judah and the nations, then the second half where the LORD Jesus Himself steps into the foreground.

> "From the vision of divine purposes (chapters 13-27) Isaiah turns to the reality of divine power. It is the task of chapters 28-37 to demonstrate that the Lord does actually rule world history and that, therefore, his as yet unfulfilled promises and purposes are sure. At two climactic points in chapters 13-27 (19:24-25; 27:13), Isaiah predicted the gathering of Egypt and Assyria into full membership of the Lord's people... To Isaiah's contemporaries this must have seemed both marvellous and unlikely – that aliens should become members, inveterate enemies friends, and imperial powers quietly submissive! Isaiah therefore offers the greatest of his interim fulfilments, a period of history in which divine sovereignty over Judah, Egypt and Assyria would be demonstrated before their very eyes... As we shall see, the occasion is that of the 'Egyptian alliance' in the days of Hezekiah. Judah is seen wilfully refusing the way of trust in the Lord for trust

in Egypt; Egypt is revealed as blustering and ultimately ineffective; and the Assyrian army, bending its colossal power to punish the rebels, is destroyed by the Angel of the Lord." (Motyer, 227).

1. A Stone in Zion – 28:1-29:24

The garlanded head of Ephraim (28:1-6)

Samaria was the capital of Ephraim and in Amos 3:12-15 and 6:1-6 we learn how they had built up the city to be a luxury palace, adorned with ivory. Sitting on top of its mountain it would have looked like a garland on the head of Ephraim. The fertility and harvest celebrations had descended into drunkenness and pride (28:1). So, the true LORD of the harvest would bring down that pride with terrible weather (verse 2) and the garland of natural glory will be trodden underfoot. When the judgment has fallen on Ephraim then it will be clear that Christ alone, the LORD Almighty, is the only glorious crown for His people. He will bring justice and strength in the Spirit and His Church will have no other wreath, no other glory, than Jesus alone.

The nonsense teachers (28:7-13)

"In modern nations the besetting temptation of religious leadership is sex. In Israel it was drink (vv7-9). The former distorts peoples' insight, but the latter does so more obviously." (Goldingay, 154).

> The priests and prophets were supposed to lead the people to Christ the LORD, but all they did was utter childish nonsense (verses 9b and 10). The alcohol had confused their thinking and though they no longer had any true wisdom we can well imagine in the materialistic hedonism of Samaria that these religious leaders might try to come up with a message of restraint and religion to fit in with the situation. But it was just nonsense. Mere rules and legalism do nothing to control sin, as was clearly demonstrated in their own lives.

The Hebrew for verses 11 and 13 is sav, asav sav lasav, kav lakav kav lakav intended to sound like the meaningless words that these prophets might speak. So, if they are willing to listen to incomprehensible messages then the Living God will give His truth to the foreign nations and then they will come to preach to them in these Gentile languages that they cannot even understand (verse 11). They had a clear message of where to find rest (verse 12), but even that clear message will sound nonsense to them (verse 13).

In 1 Corinthians 14:20-25 Paul refers us back to this passage from Isaiah to show how important it is for us to hear the Word of God in clear terms in our own language. A local Church may well have people from different nations, speaking different languages, but if the message is spoken in a generally unknown language without translation then it would be as if they were living under the judgment against Ephraim/Jerusalem, hearing the truth in an unknown foreign language.

Jesus, the solid foundation (28:14-22)

The prophets and priests made no sense, so the people had turned to the very political alliances that the LORD warned them against. The covenant with death might refer to a political agreement with Egypt. They might have seen it as a chance of life, but Isaiah simply describes it as a death agreement.[43] Yet they have tried to find refuge in a lie and a falsehood.

Right there in front of them was a true refuge, a true Rock that would give them guaranteed security in the coming crisis (verse 16). Christ the Rock is the very foundation stone of Zion, the heavenly city of the Living God. He is a 'tested stone', proven to deliver on His promises and keep His people safe. The city of God depends entirely on Him for its structure because He is both the foundation underneath and the cornerstone of the building.

The faithful saints that reject human glory and look only to Christ's glory are not thrown into the foolishness of panic but can keep a clear mind. Justice and righteousness are the test of any refuge for God's people and Egypt obviously do not have them. Just as the LORD destroyed Egypt with hail in the Exodus, so He will judge them again (verses 17-19).

---

43 It is possible that the covenant with death is meant more literally as they looked to the pagan worship of the dead to find security. Perhaps they had 'good luck charms' of bones that were supposed to keep them safe when the Assyrian invasion came or maybe they offered sacrifices (even of children) in order to satisfy the hunger of the realm of the dead (verse 15).

"The metaphor of the *bed* reflects ironically the refused resting place of verse 12. They have made their own bed and must now lie on it, but only to find that if they lie full stretch the bed is too short, and if they curl up the blanket is too narrow!" (Motyer, 234).

Just as the LORD gave His anointed king (David) great victory over his enemies in 2 Samuel 5:17-25, even as he was securing Jerusalem, so Christ would rise up against His enemies again to secure Zion, even though His enemies now are not the Philistines but the people of Judah living in Jerusalem. This work of judging His own people is "His strange work.. His alien task", yet He will do it nonetheless (verse 22).[44]

The magnificent wisdom of the LORD (28:23-29)

As we have seen, the destructive judgments of the LORD on Israel, Judah and all the nations are only a preparation for a fruitful harvest. The breaking up of the hard ground is only so that the planned crop can be produced. Each kind of crop needs its own special kind of sowing and harvesting, so this is how the LORD deals with the nations. The farmer learns how to farm from God (28:26), so the LORD knows the right methods for each nation. His plan is wonderful and His wisdom is magnificent.

As it is in a dream (29:1-8)

So, although Jerusalem (Ariel) will be humbled to the dust (29:1-4), yet the enemies that came to besiege her will themselves be destroyed by the LORD just when these enemies were already tasting their victory. Her enemies will feel as if they are just about to get all the plunder, but will actually get nothing, as if they were just dreaming of their victory (29:7-8).

Their hearts are far from me (29:9-16)

The LORD's people have chosen blindness and stupidity (as Isaiah was warned right back in chapter 6), so the LORD has confirmed their choice (29:10). He has given them over to their own hardness of heart and

---

44 "Isaiah's call to reform is based on what he knows is coming (he has heard it from the Lord; he advocates repentance not because repentance will prevent it (it is definite) but because there is no other way to prepare. The only way to flee from God is to flee to him." (Motyer, 235).

Isaiah

prevented them from understanding the prophetic words of Isaiah (29:11-12). When we turn away from the LORD it has a terrible legacy, driving us further into the darkness. Yes, the people were prepared to play at 'Church', outwardly going through the motions and pretending at 'religion' (29:13).

They have the religious traditions, which are done with all the reverence and show, yet in their hearts the people were far away from the Living God.

We can so easily deceive even ourselves as we substitute religion for reality. Jesus is always the ultimate enemy of 'religion' because religion covers over the truth about us. He wants our hearts and our lives or else He wants nothing of us at all.

In our religious delusion we imagine that the LORD can't see what is really going on in our hearts, that we can hide the truth from Him (29:15-16). We act as if we could manipulate our Maker, as if the clay could shape the potter (verse 16).

Rejoice in the Holy One of Israel (29:17-24)

The Living God is no mere idea or fantasy, so He will come down from the heavens and prove His reality. Even to those who are blind and deaf, lost in the darkness, He will bring sight and salvation (29:18). He will open blind eyes and show Himself in spite of His people's rejection of Him. Then the humble will rejoice in Him and the proud mockers will be taken away with all their social injustice (29:19-21). When His people see how the LORD has healed the blind and wayward people, giving them understanding and making them eager for instruction, then the shame of His people will be gone (29:22-24). This is the work of the LORD's hands and all the glory goes to Him.

We can never save ourselves. We can't even escape from the evil desires that control us. Only when the LORD Jesus opens our blind eyes by His Spirit do we really see who He is and what He has done for us.

2. *Woe to those who rely on Egypt* – 30:1-31:9

The great concern of these chapters is the danger of relying on Egypt for security and trying to find refuge in any merely human strength or wisdom. When human resources are seen as an alternative to the glory of Christ the LORD then judgment must come. As we have seen so many times, the pattern is judgment-gospel-judgment (judgment (30:1-17) – gospel (30:18-33) – judgment (31:1-9)).

Woe to those who look to Egypt for refuge (30:1-17)

In all these judgments against trust in Egypt we need to understand the universal power of these prophecies. In our nations, our Churches, our communities and our own individual lives we are always faced with this same basic choice: Christ as the desire of all nations or else human glory, human strength, human wisdom.

Jesus Himself declared that we must chose between God and Mammon, where Mammon is all that belongs to the glories of this passing age (Matthew 6:24).

When we make *our own* plans and decide what is best for our lives, then there is only woe for us (30:1). The plans we need are *the LORD's* and the alliance that is best for us is the one with Christ by His Spirit. The people of Judah were looking to Pharaoh and Egypt for their refuge, but there is no advantage there, only shame and disgrace (30:4-5). Remember that all the time Isaiah is giving these prophecies he is naked, showing the shame that will fall on the Egyptians when they too are led away to exile (20:1-6).

All the resources that the LORD had given to His people are carried away through the desert hardships of the Negev in order to buy the 'help' of Egypt (30:6-7). The Church wastes her blessings on useless help, on Egypt the "do-nothing" (verse 7). How this must hurt the heart of our Loving God! He gives us good things and then we use them to rebel against Him, to sinfully serve our own desires and foolish ideas.

So, Isaiah was to write out a complaint from the LORD and perhaps post it up in a public place for all to see, describing how the children of the LORD are rebellious and unwilling to listen to Him (30:8-9). They actually try to silence those who speak His Word (verses 10-11) – "Stop confronting us with the Holy One of Israel! Stop talking about Christ all the time! Stop calling us to Him when we want to go our own way!"

So, this sin of relying on Egypt and trying to silence the Word of Christ will bring disaster on them. Their alliance with Egypt will be like a wall

Isaiah

that looks strong but actually bursts apart in a moment (30:12-14). The alternative to relying on Egypt is always trusting in Christ, basking in His glory. There was still time to go another way:

> "In repentance and rest is your salvation, in quietness and trust is your strength, but you would have none of it" (30:15).

So, far from being strong they will be weak and cowardly. Even if they outnumbered the Assyrians 1000 to 1 they would still be too afraid to attack (verse 17), running away at the slightest danger.

This is so true of us in every generation. The LORD's people want security and peace, yet when we look for it apart from Him we are cursed with fear and confusion, with depression and despair. He will not share us with the gods and idols of this world.

The LORD longs to be gracious to you (30:18-33)

In spite of all the betrayal and unfaithfulness, still "the LORD longs to be gracious to you; therefore He will rise up to show you compassion. For the LORD is a God of Justice" (verse 18). Note that it is the LORD's justice that means that He will be gracious and compassionate. The idea that His justice is the opposite of His mercy comes from that pagan view of justice as an impersonal dispenser of punishment. In reality justice not only punishes the wicked but will also restores those who repent and call on the LORD.

The LORD is quick to forgive His people if only they will cry to Him – "As soon as He hears, He will answer you" (verse 19). Though they will eat and drink affliction for a time (30:20) yet after that they will learn to know their Teacher, the Holy Spirit Himself, who will guide them at all times.[45] Then all the idols of political security or pagan worship will be thrown away (verse 22).

---

45 "The period of affliction will be a time of divine self-concealment (8:17) but it will be followed by a time of direct relationship. The translation *teachers* is permissible, but the context requires the singular, which the form also allows, i.e. 'your Teacher', referring to the Lord as the law/instruction giver. This divine self-revelation will be matched by powers of receptivity, eyes to see and ears to hear." (Motyer, 250).

So, when the day of judgment comes, though it will mean slaughter and destruction for the world, yet for the Church it will mean great blessing. The Church is the moon, shining with the reflected glory of Jesus, so on that day she will shine as brightly as the sun, which shines seven times brighter (30:23-26).

Again Isaiah shows us the LORD Jesus Christ coming on the day of judgment (verses 27-30), the majestic and glorious Divine Judge judging the world and saving His people. If He can do that in the far future, He can certainly "shatter Assyria" in the immediate future (verse 31). Even while Assyria is being destroyed by the LORD, His people will be celebrating with harps and tambourines (verse 32).

> "Little did the Assyrians know that their imperial progress to (Jerusalem) (10:8-11) was their funeral procession with the pyre long since laid!" (Motyer, 253).

Woe to those who go down to Egypt for help (31:1-9)

If that is how the LORD is about to defeat Assyria, then why would the leaders of Judah ever want to make an alliance with Egypt? The only explanation is that they do not trust the LORD. They do not believe that He can defeat the Assyrians in that way.

In our day too we might imagine that military power will give us safety or perhaps that medical technology will secure our lives, yet it is the Holy One of Israel (verse 1) who alone can really help us. We might think that the world will make a good friend, but in making friends with the world we make an enemy of the Living God and He "can bring disaster" (verse 2).

If we have the world as our enemy then it can do us some damage, but if the LORD Jesus is our enemy then He can not only end our life in this passing age but also throw us body and soul into Hell itself (Matthew 10:28). The Egyptians are just human beings, but Christ is the Living God (31:3).

The LORD is a much better defender of His people than Egypt or any other ally ever could be. He is like a lion that is scared of nothing, or like birds flying overhead the LORD will pass over His people to rescue them. This reference to the Passover (31:5) is quite deliberate. In all kinds of

Isaiah

ways, Isaiah is reminding the Church of the events of Exodus when Egypt was proved to be far, far weaker than the Angel of the LORD.

3. *Your God will come* – 32:1-35:10

In the next section of our studies (chapters 36 through to 41) Christ (the Angel of the LORD) does in fact come to save Jerusalem from the Assyrian war machine. All that the LORD has promised through Isaiah about His ability to defend them will be vindicated when He actually does it before their very eyes.

So, chapters 32-35 help to prepare us for the coming of the Angel of the LORD in salvation and judgment.

The King of Righteousness (32:1-20)

We begin by looking at the Messiah-King reigning in righteousness, as prophesied back in 9:1-7 and 11:1-10. The rulers under Him embody all His principles of truth and justice. In that new creation future, there will be protection from every threat. Even the deserts will have streams of water. Living in the shadow of Christ the King will be like the cool shelter of a great Rock in a thirsty land. The NIV says "each man will be like a shelter" but the Hebrew is literally 'a man', referring to Christ the King Himself.[46]

In 6:9-10 Isaiah would face people who see but never perceive, who hear but never understand. Yet, in the kingdom of Christ the LORD, those seeing eyes and hearing ears will truly perceive and understand. The fearful mind will understand and the stammering tongue will be free to speak clearly (verse 4). The fool and the scoundrel (whose wickedness is described in verses 6-7), will no longer receive the respect that they do in this dark age.[47]

In contrast to the Messiah's future kingdom, Isaiah speaks to the women of Jerusalem about their comfortable complacence, their merriment and revelry in the condemned city of Jerusalem. This old order of sin and evil when the glory of Christ is rejected and fools and scoundrels are

---

46 King James Version – "And a man shall be as an hiding place from the wind, and a covert from the tempest; as rivers of water in a dry place, as the shadow of a great rock in a weary land."

47 "An imperfect society imperfectly accords honour. Isaiah looks forward to a true aristocracy of character." (Motyer, 258).

honoured will soon be judged and destroyed. There is no future for this sinful world order. The time of the LORD's justice dwelling and renewing the deserts will not come until the old is swept away and the Spirit is poured out from on high (verse 15). Then creation will blossom, the curse of thorns and barrenness will be gone and sin itself will be cleansed away. When the world is right with God then peace, quietness and confidence will flourish forever (verse 17). After the judgments have destroyed the cities and the forests, yet the LORD's people will live in safety with fertile crops and animals (verses 18-20).

What a glorious vision of our resurrection future! We yearn for that day of judgment because beyond it is the new creation kingdom of Christ.

Betrayal by Assyria; faithfulness from Christ (33:1-24)

Chapter 33 takes this vision forward. This prophecy was probably given in the context of 2 Kings 18:13-18 after Assyria's apparent acceptance of Hezekiah's deal. However, the attack on Jerusalem was continued as if no agreement had been reached. So, it is woe to those who destroy and betray, because there will come a time when the tables will be turned and Assyria will be betrayed and destroyed (33:1).

In contrast to these traitorous Assyrians the people of God should turn to Him asking for mercy, seeking strength from Him each morning. With the Assyrians banging on the gates, in the time of distress, the ancient Church turns to their Saviour (verse 2). Yes, right now we may suffer but in the end, the LORD's army is terrifying to the nations and the battle is over before it even began (verse 4 and Revelation 19). He brings justice to His city.

Christ alone is the sure foundation, the reliable Friend and Ally in all troubles. In Him are hidden all the treasures of wisdom and knowledge (33:6) and the key to the treasures in Him is simply to fear Him – to love Him and trust Him.

Verses 7-9 might well relate to the incidents in 2 Kings 18 when the Assyrian siege of Jerusalem carries on even though the peace envoys had tried to buy peace with the temple treasures. Verse 8 refers to the broken treaty. This treachery seems to be the final straw for the Angel of the LORD who will now arise to defend His people. When the LORD arises

Isaiah

then His consuming fire will burn away the sinners and the godless, who give birth to the tinder for the fire that consumes them.

> "The tragedy of sin is that it ruins the life of the sinner; the danger of sin is that it excites the wrath of God" (Motyer, 265).

Calling to the Gentiles far away and the Hebrew people nearby (verse 13), the LORD summons the world to acknowledge His power (verse 13)

Who can dwell in that everlasting, consuming fire of the LORD's presence (verse 14)? This refers to the fire burning on the altar that consumes each sacrifice, the fire that indicates the holy presence of the LORD yet the fire that also marks the impassable boundary between heaven and earth. Only One Person is able to cross this boundary and enter safely onto the mountain of God – Christ Himself. He alone can fulfil the demands of 33:15, as described in Psalm 15, but especially when His ascension up to the Mountain is described in Psalm 24:3-10.

Yet, and here is the glory of Jesus, He does not ascend to the heights alone. He brings His people with Him so that they may see the beauty of the King and see His glorious heavenly country (verse 17). The wicked and arrogant who are now in power, whose confusion is apparent in their confused and unintelligible speech (verses 18-19) will be taken away and forgotten.

That glorious resurrection future when we will see Jesus as He is and enjoy His renewed heavens and earth will sustain us even now as we set our hearts and minds on Him. Even now we focus on that City of God, where the river of life flows out from the throne of God. In that heavenly city of God there will be no illness and no sin (verse 24).

The LORD is angry with all nations (34:1-17)

Isaiah calls out to the whole world that the LORD's judgments will fall on all nations (verses 1-3) and even on the heavens above (verse 4). It is as if He is making a mighty sacrifice of all the world, with Edom chosen as the example for all (verses 5-7). Edom was the nation descended from Esau and perhaps for this reason typifies the problem with the world. Esau could have submitted to Jacob so easily, leading his people into the ancient Church of Israel. Instead, he lived for the moment, putting a higher value on his immediate desires. Out of that he produced a people who carried on with the ways he taught them leading to a history of conflict with the LORD's people (see 1 Samuel 14:47; 2 Samuel 8:14; 1 Kings 11:1-25; 2 Kings 8:20; 2 Kings 14:7-10; and Edom's hostility at the fall of Jerusalem in Obadiah 10-14).

Edom had so many opportunities to return to the LORD, yet consistently went their own way. They were an Abrahamic people, yet refused the true heritage of Abraham: faith in Christ.

The divine sword has slaughtered Edom as if it were a lamb or goat or bull prepared for the altar. The coming day of God will be a day of vengeance when the LORD will vindicate His people (verse 8). Recalling the destruction that fell on Sodom and Gomorrah, Edom will be turned into pitch and burning sulphur, burning night and day for ever (verses 9-10). The wild birds that feast on fallen carcasses will be the only living things left after God has applied His standard to Edom (verse 11). Hyenas and jackals will move into the deserted cities of Edom (verses 12-15). This must happen because the LORD has spoken and His Spirit will do it (verse 16).

The animals and Zion have a future on the earth, but the wicked have no place in Christ's coming kingdom.

Your God will come (35:1-10)

So, Isaiah's prophesies come to a climax and conclusion. For more than 25 chapters Isaiah has looked at the nations, Israel and Judah, always declaring the LORD's condemnation of human pride or human glory. Christ, the Holy One of Israel, is the only safe refuge; the only resting place; the only One worth having an alliance with; the only Saviour who can provide a truly secure future; the only One strong enough to conquer all the enemies.

Christ the LORD is not just for Israel and Judah, but for the whole world. His judgments fall on all the nations so that they too will know that there is no possible hope other than in Christ alone. He is the only One who can survive the judgment of the Living God. Only those who have found refuge in Jesus; only those He has rescued will enter Zion (see Psalm 87).

Before we see how Christ delivers on His promises, Isaiah continues with his vision of the new creation future. The glory of Christ the LORD would be shown in His suffering and death (as we will see in Isaiah's detailed

Isaiah

descriptions), but it was always for the joy that was set before Him, that renewed heavens and earth that would be the everlasting home of righteousness.

The earth has been under a curse of decay and futility since human sin defiled the creation at the very beginning. The creation will suffer a cosmic judgment (chapter 34), but it will only prepare it for a cosmic renewal when even the deserts and wilderness places will become fertile gardens (verses 1-3). The glory of the LORD Jesus will be seen by the earth itself, making the wilderness as glorious as Lebanon.[48]

So, with that bright future in front of us, we can keep going even now with all the struggles and pain of this passing age. As Judah faced the threat of Assyria and then later exile under the Babylonian empire, the faithful saints could gain strength and courage by reminding each other of the day when God will come to right the wrongs and resurrect His people (verses 3-4). Then all physical problems will be cured once and for all (verses 5-6). This is why the healing ministry of Jesus in the gospels is so very important. Jesus is doing more than simply dealing with the immediate physical needs around Him in Israel of 33AD. He is demonstrating who He is. He is showing the world that He is the Righteous King, the Holy One of Israel, the God of Vengeance who will do everything that the prophets said about Him – see Matthew 11:1-6.

The jackals may have moved into the cities of Edom (34:13), but the wilderness places where they used to live will become fertile, water-side landscapes (35:7).

The resurrected Church will be able to move about in complete safety in that renewed earth. The Highway of Holiness will enable anyone to travel up to Zion without any fear of lions or wicked fools. Yes, from all over the world the redeemed will flood into the city of God, whose builder and maker is God Himself, with singing – "everlasting joy will crown their heads. Gladness and joy will overtake them, and sorrow and sighing will flee away."

---

48 It is vital that we never focus on the few who trust in Christ but always on Jesus Christ Himself. We need someone who can not only sort out the mess of our own individual lives but also renew the whole creation, bring fertility to the whole earth and change the very nature of reality! There is only One who can do all this and we must always keep Him at the very centre of all our Bible study, thought and day-to-day life.

Study 5   Bible Questions

Isaiah 33:1-17

1. Verses 1, 3-4. With the Assyrian armies banging on the gates of the city and hard times ahead, Isaiah looks beyond the current troubles to the final destiny of all oppressors and wicked people. Why is it so important to always keep that final day of justice in mind?

2. Verse 2. In the hardest times, the "time of distress" how can we find the strength to face each day?

3. Verse 5. It is all too easy to keep our eyes fixed on the troubles all around us – like Peter who focussed on the waves in Matthew 14:30. What is the remedy for this?

4. Verse 6. Looking up to the King in Zion above, we are also aware of the foundation beneath our feet and the rich store of resources to get us through the time of distress. How do we unlock this rich store?

5. Verses 7-9. Isaiah describes the land of Judah and the city of Jerusalem in the coming time of distress. List the different aspects that strike so deep. Imagine facing these troubles in our own cities or nation.

6. Verses 10-12. How does the LORD exalt Himself in these verses? Is this good news or bad news, in the light of verses 7-9?

7. Verses 13-15. Think back to the words in Isaiah 29:13 with their superficial understanding and empty devotion. Describe the contrast with 33:13-14.

8. Verses 15-17. Verse 17 holds up to our view the King who we saw in verse 5. In Him there is such a glorious hope and a safe home. Consider what makes Him such a secure hope, worthy of all our trust, in the light of verses 15-16.

Isaiah

Study 5   Further Questions

1. Should Christians have anything to do with "moral campaigns" in society or politics? Is there any value in making non-Christian people behave better or making their activities illegal? Does this bring people nearer to Jesus or drive them further away?

2. In Isaiah 28:26 we learn that farmers learn their farming methods from the LORD God. What does this mean? If Christ is the Logos who upholds the whole creation, then is all true logic and knowledge from Him?

Study 5   Daily Readings

Day 1	Isaiah 28:1-29
Day 2	Isaiah 29:1-24
Day 3	Isaiah 30:1-33
Day 4	Isaiah 31:1-32:20
Day 5	Isaiah 33:1-24
Day 6	Isaiah 34:1-17
Day 7	Isaiah 35:1-10

The daily Bible readings are an opportunity to not only read through all of the material in the book under study, but also to read parts of the Bible that relate to the themes and issues that we have been considering. Wetry to make sure that we receive light from the whole Bible as we think through the key issues each week.

Pride

Isaiah

Study 6 The Glory of the Angel of the LORD: Isaiah 36:1-41:29

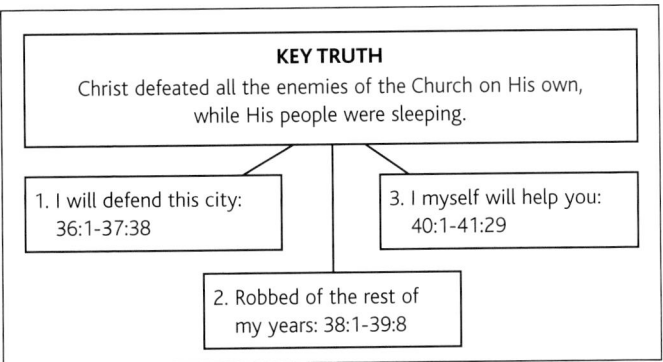

KEY TRUTH
Christ defeated all the enemies of the Church on His own, while His people were sleeping.

1. I will defend this city: 36:1-37:38
2. Robbed of the rest of my years: 38:1-39:8
3. I myself will help you: 40:1-41:29

All the way through the book of Isaiah, the prophet has told us that in the day of judgment there is only Person who can survive; only One who can handle and overcome the day of justice. Over the next few chapters Isaiah will prove that as He shows us Christ the LORD going out to face the overwhelming, apparently unstoppable power of Assyria, He does it all alone, with no help from anyone else.

When all hope is gone, then there is Christ alone in all His glory.

1. *I will defend this city* – 36:1-37:38

Isaiah doesn't give us the background to the Assyrian invasion that we find in 2 Kings 18, when Hezekiah tried to cut a deal with Sennacherib (2 Kings 18:13-16). Instead Isaiah begins the story from the point when the field commander issues an ultimatum to Jerusalem, deliberately speaking in the Hebrew language so that all the ordinary people would know what was said (Isaiah 36:11-12).

The Assyrian judgment arrives (36:1-22)

The moment of decision had arrived. For years Isaiah had been warning that the LORD was going to use the Assyrian war machine to humble Judah and Jerusalem, and now that moment had arrived. The Assyrian army had already captured the fortified cities of Judah, so many of the earlier prophecies of the Assyrian devastation will have already happened throughout Judah.[49] Now, the people were crammed into Jerusalem as the last place to hide. Hezekiah and Sennacherib would not meet directly together, so their senior assistants met together to discuss terms and the location was interesting (36:2). It was the same place that Isaiah had met with Ahaz in 7:3 (cf 22:9-11) when confronting him about his confidence in human resources. The Rabshakeh[50] wants to meet at that place to show that these preparations are of no concern to him – just as the LORD had warned through Isaiah.

The field commander's speech is very clever and spoken in the hearing of all the common people so that they would be unnerved by it. It has four key themes:

1. They cannot depend on Egypt (verses 4-7).

2. They cannot depend on the LORD (verse 7) because His places of worship have been removed.

3. Even if the Assyrians gave them horses they didn't have the manpower to use them (verse 8-9) and Egypt wouldn't deliver resources anyway.

4. The LORD had personally authorised the destruction of Judah and Jerusalem (verse 10).

What is so striking about this speech is that points 1, 3 and 4 are essentially the sort of thing that Isaiah himself has been preaching. Only in regards to the worship of the LORD in Jerusalem had he completely missed the point, although from his pagan background a reduction in places of worship would always be bad for a god. It may well have been that the Rabshakeh had heard reports of Isaiah's speech of 10:5-6 so uses it as his closing argument. Eliakim, Shebna and Joah all realise the power of the speech and want to switch the conversation to Aramaic but in brutal terms the field commander further unnerves anyone listening (verse 12).

---

49 "By the time he besieged Lachish, Sennacherib had disposed of the Tyrian and Philistine rebels and had defeated Egypt's army at Eltekeh (in Philistia, north of Lachish) on its one and only attempt to redeem its promises to the Palestinian states. Hezekiah was isolated and, politically speaking, it is no wonder that Sennacherib pocketed the Judahite tribute while at the same time determining to leave no rebels behind when he returned home." (Motyer, 277)

50 The title means something like "chief cupbearer", indicating that he was a personal assistant to Sennacherib

Isaiah

"Politicians make wars but people suffer them" (Motyer, 278). The commander goes over the heads of the officials and addresses the people directly, telling them not to trust in the LORD.

In verses 13-15 he puts the matter very directly. Hezekiah has clearly been listening to Isaiah and has told the people that they must trust in Christ the LORD in the face of the Assyrian invasion. The field commander refers to his own king as "the great king" but Hezekiah is not even referred to as a king. "Do not let Hezekiah persuade you to trust in the LORD…" Instead, verses 16-17, they should put their trust in the king of Assyria who will make peace with them and allow them to spend some time on their land before they would be deported (verse 17).[51]

In verses 18-20 the field commander puts the matter most sharply. The world is full of nations with their different gods and religions. Each of these nations and cities called out to their gods when the Assyrian army arrived, but none of these gods ever managed to stop the Assyrians from conquest. Surely they could see that they were no different to all the other nations! Surely they could see that the LORD was no more real or powerful than any of these other gods?[52]

This speech of the field commander sounds as fresh and challenging today as it did more than 2,500 years ago. The post-modern assumptions of today are implicit in his speech: there is no ultimate reality other than the truth created by human power. It is as if he had said "when real physical power in the form of military might turns up then all the 'religious' powers disappear into the fantasy world of fairies, myths and dreams."

> "Nothing can be more absurd in itself, nor a greater affront to the true and living God, than to compare him with the gods of the heathen; as if he could do no more for the protection of his worshippers than they can for the protection of theirs, and as if the God of Israel could as easily be mastered as the gods of

---

51 Notice how his words seem to echo what the LORD said back in 27:5.

52 Back in 10:8-11 Isaiah prophesied that the Assyrian king would take this view of his conquests. He would boast how he was able to get rid of the idols of the nations and would do the same to Jerusalem.

Hamath and Arphad, whereas they are vanity and a lie. They are nothing; he is the great I AM: they are the creatures of men's fancy and the works of men's hands; he is the Creator of all things." (Matthew Henry).

Isaiah's prophecy of deliverance (37:1-13)

Hezekiah cannot bear to hear Christ spoken about in this way and not only tears his clothes but goes straight to the temple (verse 1) and sent his officials, wearing sackcloth, to Isaiah and reported it all to him (verses 2-4). Finally, Hezekiah and his officials really do trust in Christ alone. The words of the field commander have the opposite effect!

> "It speaks volumes for the reality of Hezekiah's sense of sin that he bases no appeal on his own needs but only on the possibility that the Lord will stand by his own honour. In his prayer the king makes no reference to himself but recognises that the needs of the Lord's people are always a valid ground of appeal to the Lord" (Motyer, 279).

Isaiah doesn't need to pray because he is sure that the LORD will do what He has already promised (verses 5-7), and furthermore because the Assyrians blasphemed against Christ Sennacherib would end up leaving and dying in his own country.

However, before this is fulfilled Sennacherib sends another message, in the form of a letter, re-emphasising what his field commander had said – verses 8-13. In this letter a deeper challenge is given to Hezekiah: "do not let the god you depend on deceive you…" (verse 10). It is almost as if it is the devil himself who tempts Hezekiah: has God really said this? Sennacherib, like his father, the devil, thinks nothing of directly challenging the very words and promises of the Glorious God who made all things. He again tries to place the Living God on the level of the pitiful 'gods' of the nations.

Hezekiah's prayer (37:14-20)

The fact that Hezekiah spreads the letter before the LORD at the temple shows that he has thrown himself entirely on Christ the LORD, looking only to Him for answers (verse 14). His prayer begins by addressing the

Isaiah

LORD as the One who is "enthroned between the cherubim" and also over all the kingdoms of the earth; the One who made the entire heavens and the earth. In the highest heaven the Father sits on His majestic throne surrounded by hundreds of millions of incredible angelic creatures (see Daniel 7:9-10 or Revelation 4:6-8, especially Revelation 5:11-14).[53] In other words, Hezekiah is acknowledging at the beginning of his prayer that his heavenly Father, seated in heaven, who made everything, rules over all the nations and if He sends His Divine Angel, Christ the LORD, then anything is possible.

In verses 18-20 Hezekiah pleads the glory of Christ. Of course the Assyrian kings could defeat all the gods made by human hands, but what would the watching world think when he is defeated by the One, True, Living God who made us?

The LORD's reply to Assyria (37:21-35)

Hezekiah gets a very prompt reply from the LORD, through Isaiah.

First a word against Sennacherib: a young woman would be very vulnerable in military conquest, but Jerusalem is like a young woman mocking and laughing at Sennacherib (verse 22). When the king of the Assyrians blasphemed the LORD he wrote his own doom: when he challenged the glory of Christ his destruction was certain. His arrogant claims are ridiculous (verses 24-25).[54] All that was happening had been planned and predicted long before it happened – the earlier chapters of Isaiah eloquently prove this. Yes, Assyria's conquest of Judah was planned and prophesied (verses 26-27), but also the coming humiliation of Assyria (verses 28-29).

Second, a word for Hezekiah: though the Assyrian army had devastated the countryside, within three years it would be fully recovered.

---

53 On the earth this was represented in the tabernacle by the ark of the covenant within the Most Holy Place, behind the curtain. The ark of the covenant had two cherubim, one at either end, between which the Angel of the LORD would sit. Note that the Angel of the LORD would represent the Father on earth, sitting on the throne within the Most Holy Place. The role of the Son as the Great High Priest and the Lamb of God was, of course, represented by the Aaronic priests and the animal sacrifices in the tabernacle. On earth the Son represents the Father and the Levitical priests/animals represent the Son.

54 No matter how many people walk through the Nile it will never be dry and nobody can go mountaineering in a chariot!

Though many had been killed in the invasion, yet there would be enough survivors to rebuild (verse 31-32). The Assyrian army would soon be sent on its way (verse 33).

In many ways Isaiah 37:35 is a critical verse in the book. Isaiah's prophecies have claimed that the LORD is able to defend His people and that the best, military alliance is with Christ Himself, but now is the time to prove it.

The LORD now states that He will personally defend the city and save it. He will do this because of the gospel promises that He made to David long ago (see 2 Samuel 7).

The Angel of the LORD (37:36-38)

Surely this is one of the most thrilling parts of the whole Bible! Here is the day of judgment brought forward into the middle of history, a day when the Church is vindicated against all her enemies. Christ, the Angel of the LORD, went out and personally defeated the entire Assyrian army: 185,000 soldiers were killed.[55] The Church went to sleep the night before trusting in Christ, but surrounded by a vast and powerful army who were blaspheming the Name of Christ. When they woke up the next morning, with no contribution or effort from themselves at all, everything had been done for them. Christ had accomplished His work of salvation while they were sleeping!

The night is far spent and the morning is at hand for us too and soon we will also gaze out at the complete victory of Christ as we enter into the blessing of the land He has promised to give us.

As prophesied, the Assyrian army and Sennacherib had to withdraw and though Sennacherib trusted in his own god, Nisrok, yet it was not able to protect him from even his own sons (verse 38) and he was killed by the sword just as the LORD had planned (37:7).

---

55 It has been suggested that "the Angel of the LORD" here is simply a phrase meaning "an agent from the LORD" and probably referred to a plague that struck the Assyrian army. Not only does this miss the meaning of the Angel of the LORD in the rest of the Scriptures, but it misses the vital personal connection between Christ and His people. Christ Himself comes to save His people and bring judgment on His enemies, just as He did at the cross and just as He will do when He returns in glory.

Isaiah

2. *Robbed of the rest of my years* – 38:1-39:8

If we are going to understand the closing years of Hezekiah's life we must remember Isaiah 57:1-2. "The righteous perish, and no-one takes it to heart; the devout are taken away, and no-one understands that the righteous are taken away to be spared evil. Those who walk uprightly enter into peace; they find rest as they lie in death." The big question to ask as we study Isaiah chapters 38 and 39 is this: would it have been better for Hezekiah and for Judah if Hezekiah had died 15 years earlier? Yes, that's a hard question to ask, but what does Isaiah want to tell us here?

Right when Hezekiah is at the best time of his life, when he is trusting Christ more faithfully then ever before, when Christ has won this amazing battle in defence of Jerusalem, when the nation is enjoying a time of optimistic rebuilding, that is moment when Hezekiah is struck down with a fatal illness. Isaiah brings him a word from the LORD: "get ready to die".

> "Neither men's greatness nor their goodness will exempt them from the arrests of sickness and death." (Matthew Henry).

We must all be ready to die because it could come at any time.

> "Our being ready for death will make it come never the sooner, but much the easier: and those that are fit to die are most fit to live." (Matthew Henry).

Hezekiah turns to prayer with tears and the LORD has mercy on him, sending Isaiah back with a promise of 15 years more life, connecting this promise to His promise of defending the city against the Assyrians (verse 6). In 2 Kings 20:8-11 we learn that Hezekiah wanted a special sign of this extraordinary promise, so asked for the incredible miracle of the shadow on the stairway going back ten steps. It is an astounding miracle, in astronomical terms apparently much more difficult that the healing of Hezekiah, and yet the LORD is gracious to do it.[56] The same LORD who defeats the Assyrians may also heal all troubles and also give us signs of

---

56 What exactly did the LORD God do? Did He adjust the rotation of the entire earth to accomplish this so that all shadows across the whole world were also set back this distance? Or, which seems more likely, did He work a local miracle in that place to change the way the light and shadows worked in Hezekiah's room?

His care for us. Even if He does not take away all our physical troubles, still He will always give us signs of His care for us – "though I walk through the valley of the shadow of death, I will fear no evil because You are with me; your rod and your staff, they comfort me" (Psalm 23:4).

Hezekiah records this experience in his journal (verses 9-20). He is full of thanksgiving and he reflects on the way he was thinking during his crisis. He had felt that it was unfair for him to die so young (verse 10) and he felt that he could still so much (verse 11), yet his body was just like a tent that is easily pulled down and his life like a thread in a loom that is easily broken. There is no permanence to our life in this world, in this age.

From the moment we are born we must be ready to die and if we have not prepared for that we will not be able to cope with it when the time arrives. Even as in his suffering he still looked to the LORD, asking for His help (verses 13-14). It is glorious how often the LORD draws especially close to His people when they are suffering and in their final illness.

After he was healed Hezekiah pledges to live always with a new humility. He could see how this good had come from the suffering (verses 15-17). The LORD had not only restored him physically but also spiritually (17b).

To have our sins forgiven is the greatest comfort of all in life or death. We must all die sooner or later and if our sins our not forgiven then death will swallow us up and never let us go. Without Christ we go do to the pit (verse 18), into Sheol with no possibility of ever praising or trusting the LORD God ever again. It is given to us once to die and then the judgment (Hebrews 9:27). Jesus promised us that when we trust Him then we will never really die; that even though we physically die, yet death will not touch us!

> John 8:51 – "I tell you the truth, if anyone keeps my word, he will never see death."

However, though Hezekiah was full of thanksgiving, he did not always walk humbly before the LORD.

> "Thanksgiving is good, but thanks-living is better."
> (Matthew Henry).

Babylon was the up and coming rival to Assyria and when the king of

Isaiah

Babylon heard that Hezekiah had recovered from his illness, he sent gifts and envoys to Jerusalem.[57] Without consulting the LORD through Isaiah, Hezekiah showed everything in the whole kingdom of Judah to the Babylonian ambassadors. Presumably out of pride he wanted them to marvel at all the wonderful things he possessed, yet the Babylonians did not forget this visit and just over 100 years later the Babylonians returned to capture Judah and Jerusalem.[58] In doing this Hezekiah was storing up trouble for later generations (verses 5-7), though he didn't seem to care about this (verse 8).

This is the tragedy of Hezekiah. At the siege of Jerusalem his trust in Christ the LORD is so strong, yet in those final 15 years he seems to undo so much of the good that he had done. Again, we need to ask, would it have been better for Hezekiah to have been spared the troubles of his extra years?

3. *I myself will help you* – 40:1-41:29

Hezekiah was worried only about peace and security in his own lifetime, but Christ has a much bigger vision of comfort for all His people in every age (40:1). Jerusalem had been through hard times and Christ had saved her, but He would always have comfort for His people. He commands that this comfort be spoken tenderly to His people.

How? If the judgment of the Living God would destroy all people, even the remaining tenth (6:13), then what comfort could there be? The answer is given right away (40:2) and it is the glorious answer that will be spelled out over the remaining chapters of Isaiah. The sin of the Church has been paid for: there is no guilt against her and no punishment to suffer.

How can this be? Christ Himself will do this. He is the Servant who will suffer the punishment instead of His people. He will take their sins upon Himself.

Isaiah gets our attention fixed on the coming of the Messiah with this

---

57 It seems very likely that the real interest of the Babylonians was how Judah had managed to inflict such a massive defeat on the great Assyrian army.

58 The first siege and fall of Jerusalem by the Babylonians was in 597BC, then again in 587BC.

famous prophecy of John the Baptist (40:3-4). When Christ is born, when Immanuel is born of the virgin (Isaiah 7:14; 9:6; 11:1-2), a wilderness prophet will prepare the way for Him.

We have heard so much about the glory of the LORD throughout the book so far. The glory of humanity is not allowed to stand against the glory of Jesus, yet what exactly is this glory of the LORD Jesus Christ? Glory is the revelation or manifestation of who somebody really is. Their glory is the shining out of who they are. For us sinful humans all our glory can only ever be a revelation of our pride, our greed, our idolatry. Yet, Immanuel would come and show *His* glory to "all people" (verse 5).

How would He do this? That is our urgent question. Isaiah will show us that the true and ultimate revelation of the glory of the LORD will come when He dies as the sacrifice for His people. The apostle John takes up Isaiah's "glory of the Cross" in his own biography of Jesus. The night before He was crucified Jesus prayed "Father the hour has come. Glorify you Son, that your Son may glorify you" (John 17:1-5).

In these chapters Isaiah is going to show us human mortality and weakness, but also the self-sacrificial grace and kindness of Christ the LORD in all that He does for His Church, right up to the creation of a new heavens and earth.

So, the voice is told to declare that although all human life passes away like weeds, yet the Word of God, Christ and His Truth, are the solid Rock that is the eternal foundation for His people (verses 6-8). Notice that although the Spirit or Breath of the LORD is the one who gives life to all (Psalm 104:30), yet He is also the one who takes it from us (verse 7).[59]

Yes, the gospel preachers coming to Zion must announce Immanuel with a shout – "Here is your God. He is coming with all His power and authority" (verses 9-10). Immanuel comes as the Good Shepherd who personally loves and cares for His sheep (40:11).

This tender Shepherd is at the same time the One through whom all things were made. Christ is such a glorious and mysterious Person: both

---

59 "The Spirit (*the breath of the LORD*) who is 'the LORD, and giver of life' (Ps. 104:30) is also the Lord, and giver of death. There is a factor of divine judgment at work in the world, a visitation of death, for *breath* is 'spirit'". (Motyer, 301)

Isaiah

the Suffering Servant and the One who holds the heavens and the earth together; both the One who carries the lambs and the One to whom the nations of the world are as nothing (verse 17). He alone can fathom the Spirit of God and advise the Most High with knowledge and understanding (verse 14). The One Living God needs no other gods for permission or insight. The Father, Son and Spirit are all sufficient.

Who or what is even comparable to this Majestic Living God: Father, Son and Holy Spirit?

The nations trust in their idols, their man-made gods and mythological beings (40:19-20), but the Living God cannot be compared to such things. He sits enthroned in the highest heavens, far above the 'powers' of this passing age. He can overcome any of the great empires as if they were nothing, merely by blowing on them (40:21-24). The stars in the heavens may be worshipped by the pagans (verse 26), but they were all made and named by the Holy One of Israel, Christ the LORD.

The Church may sometimes feel as if the LORD has forgotten them, that He doesn't see what has happened to them (verse 27), but Christ is the Everlasting God who never gets distracted or tired. His plans may not be clear to us but that is simply because His understanding is too deep for us to grasp (verse 28).

The end of the chapter is one of the glorious promises of the whole Bible. Whether we are in hard times or not, whether we are refugees going into exile or we are in relative comfort, we do not trust in our own strength or resources.

We always wait on the LORD and then He will give us His own strength. We might think that we are young enough to trust to our own strength or we might fear that we are too old or weary to go on, yet as we hope in Christ He will renew our strength.

Notice in verse 31 how it moves to ever more slow and steady ways of travelling, from *soaring* with the eagles to *running* without weariness and finally *walking* without fainting. The key is endurance: slow and steady and consistent living day by day. It is not what we do in the times of great excitement, but what we do in the constant pattern of daily labour that really counts.

Who controls world history? – 41:1-29

Turning from comfort for the Church, the LORD now issues a challenge to the nations of the world: "Who controls world history? Who can determine or predict world history?" – see verses 1-4 and verses 21-29.

The islands are challenged to renew their strength from their own resources (as opposed to what the LORD does for His people in 40:31). In 41:2-3 the LORD describes a leader of an empire coming from the east, a man who conquers all kinds of nations as he goes. At this stage Isaiah does not reveal who the LORD is speaking about, though in 44:28 and 45:1 he is explicitly named as Cyrus, the future leader of the Persian empire more than 100 years later. The LORD is the first and the last, the One who created all things and the One who brings everything to the destiny He planned from the start (verse 4).

The nations of the world are lost and fearful as they consider the events of history so they turn to their home-made idols to comfort them (41:5-7). This may take form of actual pagan idols or more commonly the money and possessions we have accumulated (see Ephesians 5:5).

The Church can face history with calm and stability as she trusts in her LORD and Saviour. The chosen people of the Living God, trusting in Christ just as Abraham did (verse 8), do not need to fear (verse 10).

Note how the Church can even be called "my servant" and "chosen" though they are the key titles to introduce Christ Himself in 42:1-2. Throughout the Bible there is such a close relationship between Christ and His Church: He shares His righteousness and holiness, His wisdom and power, His Spirit and His life. We will see in the coming chapters of Isaiah how he will use the title 'my servant' to refer to both Christ in some passages and the Church in other passages. It is a brilliant move whereby the sinful blindness of the Church is joined to the perfect righteousness of Christ, so that when we read that He has carried our sins and sicknesses we have already seen that happening as we have been bound together with Him under the titles of Servant.

The Holy One of Israel is with them by His Spirit to strengthen them and uphold them through all of history.

Isaiah

There are three examples of this: hostile enemies (41:11-13; personal weakness (41:14-16); and difficult circumstances (41:17-20).

Notice the constant reassurance through the chapter: "Do not fear". The events of history and our own lives can easily make us afraid yet Christ constantly tells us not to be afraid: He is with us and will never let us go. He has a glorious future for us when all the enemies are gone, when our weakness will be replaced with joy, when the whole world will be free of all suffering.

The enemies of the Church are nothing (verses 11 and 12) and have no future. In the end they will disappear. Though we may feel as weak and helpless as a worm, yet in the end we will judge the world as we glory in the Holy One of Israel (verses 14-16). *Now* we face physical suffering, but *soon* we will enjoy a new creation where everything is as it should be (verses 17-20).

That is the future as predicted and promised by the Holy One of Israel, the true King over all (verse 21). So, the challenge to the nations and their gods/idols is this: what can they make of history? Can they set out the future like this?[60] Can they explain the past properly (verse 23)? Can they make sense of what has already happened?

Even if they can't do that, then perhaps they can do something, some act in history that "we will be dismayed and filled with fear" (verse 23). However, anyone who trusts in a god or idol who cannot do anything is as useless as such gods (verse 24). The nations have no-one to explain history (verse 28) and are dragged into the evil behaviour of these useless gods.

> "The idolator is involved in fraudulent religion, the trouble it brings and the personal iniquity of false worship" (Motyer, 318).

Revelation 5 picks this theme up when no-one can unlock the meaning of history other than Christ, the Lamb who was slain. Only Jesus, through His death and resurrection, is able to explain the meaning of history.

---

60 One of truly quaint surprises that one comes across in the study of Isaiah is the number of modern commentaries that assert that a different later 'Isaiah' must have written the prophecies dealing with Babylon or the Persian empire because they are so accurate! The great claim of Isaiah is that the LORD predicts history but the idols cannot, but if these words were written by a much later 'prophet' who is writing 'prophecies' after the facts, then he is not only a liar but a fool!

Once again the challenge is focussed on the coming figure from the north (verse 25).[61] The proof of God is His ability to tell the future and bring salvation.[62] Religion and philosophy is just so much opinion and speculation, but the Living God through Christ tells us what the future holds, acts for us in the present and makes sense of the past.

---

61 The Hebrew for "calls on my name" may equally well be understood as "proclaims my name" through his actions in history.

62 The apostle Peter puts the matter as bluntly as this: "Through Jesus you believe in God" (1 Peter 1:21). Luke begins his gospel by stating that he is going to present the life of Jesus as the fulfilment of the prophecies so that his readers may "know the certainty" of Jesus. We know that Jesus is true because He is and did all that was prophesied about Him. He brought salvation, which only the Living God can do.

Isaiah

Study 6 Bible Questions

Isaiah 40:1-14

1. Verse 1-2. Isaiah 39:5-7 announces that though the Assyrian armies have retreated, the Babylonian armies will come to take the people away to exile. How can Isaiah 40:1 follow on from that? What possible comfort could there be in the light of that terrible prophecy?

2. Verse 3. Though the people might be in exile, though they might feel they are in the wilderness or the desert, yet how does this new prophecy give deep comfort and hope? (See Mark 1:1-3).

3. Verse 4. Why do valleys need to be raised up and mountains made low? What is this image telling us about the coming of God?

4. Verse 5. Think about the situation of Isaiah and the ancient Church, surrounded by hostile nations and all kinds of mere 'religion'. How does this verse deal with that?

5. Verses 6-7. This might sound like an unpromising message to announce to the world, but why is this such an important truth for us all to take to heart? What does this tell us about human glory?

6. Verse 8. Is there any hope for mortal human beings? Compare the hope of this verse to the end of verse 5, and consider who the Word of God is.

7. Verse 9. It is almost as if the prophecy of the coming LORD God has already happened and it is time to preach His arrival. Why would Isaiah do this? Wasn't Christ the LORD still hundreds of years into the future?

8. Verse 10. What does this Sovereign LORD bring with Him? (Consider also verses 12-14) Why is this important?

9. Verse 11. How does Christ the LORD use all that power and ability?

Study 6   Further Questions

1. The different nations of the world have all kinds of gods or philosophies (whether atheistic or not), in the way that the Assyrian field commander said, yet in the end is it nothing but military and economic power that shape history? What is the best answer in our day for that line of thought? In that day it was the historical presence of Christ, the Angel of the LORD, that answered the Assyrian field commander, so do we too always need to make our stand on the historical reality of Jesus Christ rather than abstract and philosophical ideas?

2. How do we both celebrate life as the wonderful, gracious gift of the Living God yet also always be ready to die? The fear of death grips people more strongly than ever and the obsession with health and long life is a central concern in the culture. How do we get the right balance so that we are calm and even happy to go to wait with Jesus when He calls us?

Study 6   Daily Readings

Day 1	Isaiah 36:1-22
Day 2	Isaiah 37:1-20
Day 3	Isaiah 37:21-38
Day 4	Isaiah 38:1-22
Day 5	Isaiah 39:1-8
Day 6	Isaiah 40:1-31
Day 7	Isaiah 41:1-29

Isaiah

Study 7   The Glory of the Servant: Isaiah 42:1-48:22

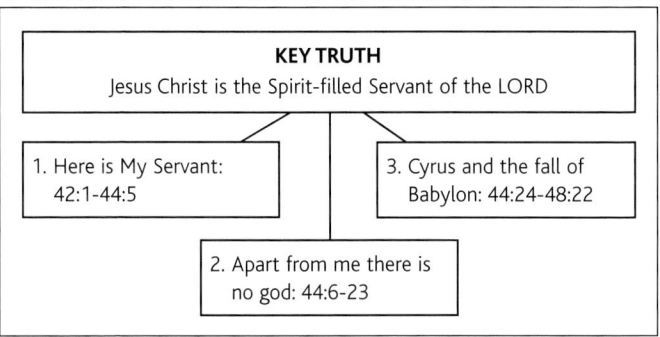

"The Prophet appears to break off abruptly to speak of Christ, but we ought to remember what we mentioned formerly in expounding another passage, (Isaiah 7:14,) that the prophets, when they promise anything hard to be believed, want to immediately afterwards mention Christ; for in Him are ratified all the promises which would otherwise have been doubtful and uncertain. "In Christ," says Paul, "is Yea and Amen." (2 Corinthians 1:20.) For what relationship can we have with God, unless the Mediator come between us? We undoubtedly are too far alienated from His majesty, and therefore could not be partakers either of salvation or of any other blessing, but through the kindness of Christ." (John Calvin, *Commentary on Isaiah*)

1. Here is My Servant – 42:1-44:5

Jacob's King had issued a challenge to all the nations back in 41:21 and now we are urged to consider this Divine King (42:1). God the Father, the One who initiated the creation of all things through Christ (see Revelation 4:11) points our attention to His Beloved Son, His Chosen Servant in whom He delights.[63]

---

63 Bernard Duhm wrote a commentary on Isaiah in 1892 suggesting that this passage along with three others (49:1-6; 50:4-9 & 52:13-53:12) were distinct "Servant Songs" that were originally quite separate from where they are now found. "Unfortunately Duhm's separation of these four passages from their context has exponentially increased the difficulty of interpreting them. His suggestion has led to a dead end and must be buried…" (Goldingay, 238).

Throughout the book of Isaiah we have learned so much about Christ. To pick just a few examples, we saw the wonderful prophecies of His birth in chapters 7-9 and then we saw how He would judge and renew the whole world in the power of the Spirit in chapter 11. We saw how everyone would fall under the judgment of God, but the Holy One of Israel could provide a refuge for His people even through the final judgment. Chapter 32 showed us this Righteous King who would open the blind eyes and unstop the deaf ears. We were told in chapter 35 that He was going to come to heal all His people and draw them to Zion in that new creation. Then at the end of chapter 37 we saw Him arrive on the scene to defend Jerusalem and judge His enemies right on the stage of history before the watching world.

The Father takes such pride in His glorious Son. In the biographies of Jesus there are three occasions when the Father publicly declares His delight in His Spirit-filled Son: at His baptism (Matthew 3:17; Mark 1:11; Luke 1:22); at His transfiguration (Matthew 17:5; Mark 9:7; Luke 9:35); and when He rode on a donkey to Jerusalem (John 12:28).

The Messiah who was so clearly described in Isaiah 11:1-5 is described in the same terms here, as the Spirit-filled servant who brings justice to the nations.[64] We have seen the ability of Christ, the Angel or Servant of the LORD, to bring destruction when He comes in judgment (37:36-37), but we see here the qualities He would display when He was born of the virgin, coming as the lowly, humble Servant. He would not make a big noise about Himself, as Matthew points out when reminding us of this prophecy in Matthew 12:18. He is slow to anger and abounding in compassion so that He will help those who are broken or bruised, ready to give up (verse 3).

From verse 5 we listen in as the Father speaks to the Son, sending Him as His Servant to do His will. These words of Scripture must have been so

---

64 One of the curious features of some modern studies of Isaiah is the fashion for following the Ethiopian eunuch in Acts 8:34, and wondering who the Servant might be that Isaiah is talking about! As the eunuch was studying Isaiah 53 he wondered if it was speaking of Isaiah himself or someone else, so Philip took the time to exegete Isaiah, showing that the prophecies were describing Jesus. It is incredible how many apparently serious commentaries seem puzzled as to who Isaiah is speaking about. Perhaps Philip should have written a commentary of his own!

Isaiah

precious to Jesus as He grew up because as He read this prophecy it must have almost felt like He was back in heaven with His Father speaking directly to Him. The Father tells Him that He has been called in righteousness (verse 6): that His position as Messiah and King and Priest is as it should be. The Father will hold His hand, guiding Him and protecting Him in all He does. Through the Bible (Genesis 6:18; 9:9; 15:8; 17:2-21; Exodus 2:24 etc) we have heard of the covenant that was given to the Church, whether from the time of Adam, Noah, Abraham, Moses or David. In those examples they are invited to be part of the covenant, but here Christ is Himself the covenant.

Christ is the Mediator between God and humanity, between heaven and earth.[65]

Yet, Christ is the covenant not only for the ancient people of Israel but also for the whole world, a light for the Gentile nations, opening blind eyes and setting us free from our dark dungeons of sin and alienation from God. This is the prophecy that Simeon remembered in Luke 2:32.

Isaiah 42:8 is so important. The LORD God will not yield His glory to another and yet He is happy to share His glory with His Son. The Father, Son and Spirit are together the one LORD God (see Deuteronomy 6:4). The LORD had challenged the nations with their gods to declare something new, but can they announce anything so wonderful as this glorious prophecy of Christ? (Verse 9)

In the light of this presentation of Christ the whole world is called to worship and praise (verses 10-13), including Kedar, the firstborn of Ishmael (verse 11) and from Sela of the Moabites (see Isaiah 16:1). Christ is ready for action (verse 13) and declares that He has been waiting so long to begin His work. He will turn the world upside down and lead the spiritually blind from all over the world in ways that they never dreamed

---

65 "It may be objected, "Why is Christ appointed to a covenant which was ratified long before? For, more than two thousand years before, God had adopted Abraham, and thus the origin of the distinction was long previous to the coming of Christ." I reply, the covenant which was made with Abraham and his posterity had its foundation in Christ; for the words of the covenant are these, "In thy seed shall all nations be blessed." (Genesis 22:18.) And the covenant was ratified in no other manner than in the seed of Abraham, that is, in Christ, by whose coming, though it had been previously made, it was confirmed and actually sanctioned." (Calvin on Isaiah 42:6)

of, making the darkness into light and the rough places smooth (verses 14-16). Yet, for those who reject the glory of Jesus and stay with their pitiful idols there is nothing but shame (verse 17).

The blind and deaf servant (42:18-25)

Christ, the Servant of the LORD, is so glorious in every way and yet He shares His name and His life with the blind and deaf that He comes to save. Yes, His people are also called to be the servants of the LORD, even though they are so blind and deaf, so hard-hearted and sinful. Christ is happy to share the name of "servant" with His people – even as in Isaiah 8:18 He was happy to call them His own family. Of course, Isaiah is preparing us for chapter 53 when we are told how Christ takes on all the sin of His people and bears our punishment.

In verses 21-25 we learn how the LORD pours out His anger on His blind, deaf and stubborn people – "He poured out on them His burning anger". It was not enough and still they were not healed.

Christ the Redeemer (43:1-44:5)

But, the Servant will not abandon the servant: the divine Servant will not abandon the sinful servant Israel that He shares His name and life with.

Throughout the book we have seen how He is the only one who can stand before the angry judgment of the Living God. He alone is the Holy One of Israel.[66] All of Israel may find shelter in that one Holy One in the presence of God. Having laid out the condemnation against us in 42:18-29 He now tells us not to fear because He has redeemed us. Thinking back to the judgment of the world by the flood or passing through the waters of death, "when you pass through the waters, I will be with you…"

In the same way, when we face that consuming fire that surrounds the Living God, that would surely consume the whole creation, "when you walk through the fire, you will not be burned; the flames will not set you ablaze." Just as Christ stood in the burning bush when He commissioned Moses (Exodus 3:1-6), so He stands in the fire to give us safe passage. Why? How can He do this? (Verse 3) – "I am the LORD your God, the Holy One of Israel, your Saviour".

---

66 Notice how often Christ is referred to as the "Holy One" in this chapter.

Isaiah

Reminding them of their deliverance in the Exodus, He says that all the nations of the world including Egypt and Cush (verses 3-4) are not worth anything to Him compared to His Church.[67] From every point on the compass He will gather the Church to Himself, from every nation (verses 5-7). The gods of the nations are unable to produce anything like Christ the LORD! (Verses 8-13). Those pagan gods and idols cannot bring salvation. Though there may be demons and devils who masquerade as 'gods' yet in the true sense of the Creator and Saviour (verse 10) "before me no god was formed, nor will there be one after me."

The true test of deity is revelation and salvation. Philosophers and religious thinkers may talk about their gods in highly abstract terms, yet how can we know if any of them really exist? A philosopher, from any religion, may speak of an "Ultimate Being" yet which, if any, of these beings really have any being at all? The Living God lays down the challenge here: have they produced a revelation of history before it happens and have they been able to save their people from sin and death?

So, if the test of deity is the ability to predict the future, what evidence does the LORD offer? Isaiah looks ahead beyond the threat of the Assyrian empire to a hundred years in the future when the Babylonians would conquer Israel and Judah (verses 13-15). Just as He gave them an exodus from Egypt, so He will make an exodus from Babylon too (verses 16-17). Yet, they do not need to constantly look back to what happened at the time of Moses, because He is doing glorious things in Christ for them now (verses 18-21).

Yet, His people have not earned this love and redemption. They have given Him nothing but sin and rebellion. They have not even brought the sacrifices of the Law as they should (verses 22-24). So, how or why has He saved them?

"I, even I, am He who blots out your transgressions, *for my own sake*, and remembers your sins no more" (verse 25).

---

67 "The Lord takes such care of all believers (1 Peter 5:7) that he values them more highly than the whole world. Although, therefore, we are of no value, yet let us rejoice in this, that the Lord sets so high a value upon us, and prefers us to the whole world, rescues us from dangers, and thus preserves us in the midst of death." (Calvin)

Right from the time of Adam there has always been sin (43:26-28). Even the leaders sent to help were sinful and rebellious. Yet, the LORD still calls Jacob His servant (44:1). Even in all our sin, in all our mess, He still tells us not to be afraid. Not only will He bring refreshment to His people, but, having forgiven their sin, He will pour out His Spirit on them (44:3) and they will rejoice in the fact that they know that they belong to the LORD (44:5).

"Hitherto the Prophet has spoken metaphorically, but now expresses his meaning plainly without any figure of speech… It means that out of all nations the Lord will gather his people, and will bring into his Church those who were formerly strangers, and will raise up and enlarge his Church, which formerly appeared to be reduced to nothing; for all shall flock to her from every quarter, and shall wish to be enrolled in the number of believers, as it is also said, "Behold Philistia, Tyre, and Ethiopia; that man was born there." (Psalm 87:4.)" (Calvin).

2. *Apart from me there is no god – 44:6-23*

The challenge to the pagan gods and the religions of the world becomes ever more intense and focussed. Christ stands in the centre of world history, having personally defeated the Assyrian army as He personally led His people out of Egypt long ago. He is looking forward to His birth, life, death, resurrection, ascension and final triumphant glory: He is the first and the last, the true King above all kings, the Redeemer. He has grown weary of all the man-made religions and idols and philosophies: "apart from me there is no God… No, there is no other Rock…" (see 1 Corinthians 10:4).

Verses 9-20 is one of the great classic pieces in the whole of world literature. Isaiah examines the whole industry of idol worship, from the skilled workers who make the objects of worship, right through to the fools who worship them. Whereas the Living God made humanity in His own image, after the likeness of Christ, yet the idol makers shape their gods in their own image (verse 13). The glory of humanity is that we are made in the image of God, yet these idols are, at best, lifeless copies of copies!

There is genuine humour in this devastating critique: the blacksmith's mighty arm makes his god, but he gets too tired to carry on; the carpenter lights a fire, bakes some bread and then out of the remainder

Isaiah

makes a god and asks it to save him. Nobody is thinking clearly about what they are doing (verses 18-20).

Yet, this comes so close to our own hearts. How many of us believe that our lives would be good if only we had a dream house in the country or a new car or a more entertainment or just more money? When we feel low do we also turn to "retail therapy" to make us feel better? The alcohol we brew; the merchandise we make with human hands; the clothes we buy; the "lifestyle" we envy: all of this is the worship of human skill. In all these ways we are asking mere creatures to save us, to do the work of God the Rock. When we look to the creatures rather than the Creator, to passing things rather than Christ Himself, then we are claiming that there is another god alongside the LORD Almighty, that there is something worthy of our worship or trust other than the Holy One of Israel.

Yet, Christ still calls to His Church (verses 21-23). He has taken away our sins so that we never need to be afraid. It is in salvation, in the Cross, that He displays His glory at maximum strength – "the LORD has redeemed Jacob, He displays His glory in Israel" (verse 23b). Yes, this great salvation would also include His care for them in face of the Assyrians in the short term and the Babylonians in the longer term, but beyond all that, the heavens and the earth must sing for joy that our sins have been taken away and we can return to the LORD Himself. It is wonderful that He gives us so many blessings in this life and in the new creation to come, but all of them fade away compared to the fact that He gives us *Himself* and calls us to come to Him.

> "...that work which he had aroused all to admire is the redemption of the Church, and declares that the glory of God shall shine forth in it illustriously. Besides, it is proper to remember what I formerly remarked, that here not only does he celebrate the return of the people to their native country, but the end is also included; for they would be "redeemed" from the captivity in Babylon on this condition, that God should at length collect under one head a Church taken out of the whole world" (Calvin).

3. *Cyrus and the fall of Babylon* – 44:24-48:22

Cyrus, the LORD's appointed man (44:24-45:25)

Now the Redeemer LORD does more than simply issue a challenge to the gods, idols and philosophies. Having created everything He can do with it just what He wants and He deliberately messes up the predictions of false prophets[68] and "overthrows the learning of the wise and turns it into nonsense" (44:25). Whenever we trust to our own wisdom or intelligence we provoke the anger of the Living God. In fact our heavenly Father takes pleasure in hiding the truth from those who think themselves to be clever as Jesus said in Matthew 11:25-27.

> "I praise you, Father, Lord of heaven and earth, because you have hidden these things from the wise and learned, and revealed them to little children. Yes, Father, for this was your good pleasure. All things have been committed to me by my Father. No one knows the Son except the Father, and no one knows the Father except the Son and those to whom the Son chooses to reveal him."

The astrologers and wise men of Assyria and Babylon may think they know the future, but the LORD gives a very specific prophecy here, not only stating that even after the exile Jerusalem will be rebuilt and furthermore a leader named Cyrus would make this happen. It is an incredible and wonderful prophecy.[69] Given that Christ has made the accuracy of prophecy the basis of His authenticity over against all other 'gods' and 'idols' then a prophecy of this level of detail and accuracy is clearly important.

---

68 It may be that Isaiah is looking forward to the time when the Church would be in exile in Babylon and would need confidence when surrounded by the very sophisticated wise men of that ancient empire. "The Prophet expressly added this, because Babylon surpassed other nations not only in the force of arms, and in troops and resources, but likewise in some remarkable sagacity, by which she appeared to penetrate even to heaven. What injury could befall those who foresaw at a distance future events, and could easily, as was commonly supposed, ward off imminent dangers? The astrologers, who were celebrated among them, foretold all events..." (Calvin). In the book of Daniel the Babylonian astrologers were considered so wise and yet the LORD God will make them look foolish.

69 "Such a detailed prediction has, of course, excited adverse comment and is taken to be a ground for insisting that these prophecies must be dated after Cyrus began his victorious rise. But first, if the fact of predictive prophecy is accepted, we are not in a position to set limits on its exercise... We may say that we do not believe it, but we are not at liberty to deny what it affirms." (Motyer, 355). Note that in 1 Kings 13:2 we have another example of a prophecy giving the name of a future leader.

Isaiah

Furthermore, Cyrus would be a kind of downpayment or guarantee of the birth of Immanuel Himself. The great promise, from the beginning of the Bible, is always about Christ Himself. Yet, in the hard times of the coming years when exile to Babylon happens and when the waiting seems long they would see that the prophecy concerning Cyrus came true and therefore they would be even more sure of waiting for Christ Himself. For this reason in 45:1 the LORD even refers to Cyrus as "His messiah" – showing that the coming of Cyrus was to be understood as a sample of the coming of the True Messiah when He would be born of the virgin.[70]

So, Cyrus would subdue nations and turn the world upside down. He would gain all kinds of treasures, so that Cyrus himself might come to know the LORD (verses 1-3).[71] Yet, this blessing of Cyrus is for the sake of the Church (verse 4). The LORD is interested in His Church around the whole world (verse 6) gathering people from all nations in to know Him, that He is the LORD and that all the religions, gods and idols of the world are empty.

BUT, the real objection here might be: why does the LORD use a pagan king in this way? How can He make use of Gentile people for the sake of His Church? What have all these pagan and idolatrous nations got to do with the Church of the Living God?

This is the same objection that people would later raise against the Gentiles joining the Church in the book of Acts. When Paul answers this in Romans 9 he quotes from this very chapter of Isaiah.[72] All things are in the LORD's hands, even the coming wars and conquests: He is sovereign

---

[70] "It might be thought strange that he calls Cyrus his Anointed; for this is the designation which was given to the kings of Israel and Judah, because they represented the person of Christ, who alone, strictly speaking, is "the Lord's Anointed"… In the person of David a kingdom had been set up, which professed to be an image and figure of Christ; and hence also the prophets in many passages call him "David," and "the Son of David." (Ezekiel 37:24, 25.) … Thus God deigns to call him his "Anointed," not by a perpetual title, but because he discharged for a time the office of Redeemer; for he both avenged the Church of God and delivered it from its enemies. This office belongs peculiarly to Christ; and this ordinary appellation of kings ought to be limited to this circumstance, that he restored the people of God to the enjoyment of liberty. This should lead us to observe how highly God values the salvation of the Church, because, for the sake of this single benefit, Cyrus, a heathen man, is called "the Messiah," (Calvin, Commentary)

[71] Though in verse 4 and 5 we see that Cyrus would be a pagan who does not acknowledge the LORD.

[72] In Romans 9 Paul is answering those who are concerned about God's promises to Israel so Paul explains that not all genetically Jewish people are part of the Church/Israel – whereas Gentile people who trust in Christ do in fact become members of Israel. The Potter can do just what He wants with His clay!

over the light and the darkness, prosperity and disaster (verse 7). Over all creation the LORD is ruler (verse 8). If He chooses to use or even save Gentile people then He has a perfect right to do so. He can do whatever He wishes to do with anything or anybody He chooses. We are mere clay in His hands (verses 9-10) so how can we question what He is doing with us? If He wishes to make use of Cyrus, then how dare any of us question Him? (Verses 10-11). Having made all humanity, and the whole expanse of heaven, why should He not raise up Cyrus or in fact bring people from Egypt and Cush into the family of Zion? (Verses 13-14).

> Verse 15 "could have been spoken by the new converts, amazed at the revelation of a God who had never previously attracted their attention. Alternatively, it could be a comment from Israel in the light of events: how concealed indeed are the purposes of God when the enforced submission of Israel to the Gentile Cyrus is but a passing veil over the ultimate truth of Gentile submission to Israel! Who but the Lord could bring the Gentiles to Israel by appearing to do the reverse?" (Motyer, 364).

The makers and worshippers of idols will be put to shame, but all who seek for the LORD will find Him (verses 16-21). Refusing to be questioned by anyone, refusing to be limited to the people of Israel and Judah alone, the LORD declares "turn to me and be saved, all you ends of the earth; for I am God, and there is no other" (verse 22).

In fact, every knee will bow and every tongue will confess (verse 23) – that Jesus Christ is LORD (when Paul quotes this in Philippians 2:10-11). All the children of Israel, from whatever nation or background, who make their boast in Christ and will find salvation in Christ (verse 25).[73]

---

73 "…the remnant of adoption were always the true and lawful Israel; and although they were few in number, yet they were the first-born in the Church. Besides, all those among the Gentiles who had been ingrafted into that body began also, as we have formerly seen, to be accounted children of Abraham. One shall say, I belong to Jacob; another shall subscribe with his band, I am a descendant of Israel." (Isaiah 44 5.) And on this ground *we are now reckoned the genuine Israel of God, though we are not the descendants of Israel*. The Prophet therefore added this, both that the Jews might not think that the Lord's covenant had failed, and that they might not boast of their birth and despise the Gentiles. All are the seed of Israel. He extends this seed farther, that they may not suppose that it ought to be limited to the family of Abraham; for the Lord gathers his people without distinction from among Jews and Gentiles, and here he speaks universally of the whole human race." (Calvin).

Isaiah

The gods of Babylon (46:1-13)

The great empire at the border in Isaiah's day was Assyria, but one day it would be the rising power of Babylon (and in fact Babylon was a force to be reckoned with even in the earlier days). Furthermore, Babylon would invade and defeat both Israel and then Judah, taking the top people into exile. Having spoken of Cyrus who would set them free from that captivity, Isaiah focusses on the Babylonian gods, especially Bel and Nebo (46:1). They might claim to be powerful and wise, but their images are carried around by animals and when Cyrus defeats Babylon they will be unable to prevent these statues being taken as plunder (verse 2).

By contrast the LORD God doesn't need to be carried by anybody. In fact, He is the one who carries His own people (verses 3-4). How can Christ the LORD be compared to man-made idols who cannot save? (Verses 5-7). We must always remember, just as they needed to in their day, all that Christ has actually done in the concrete world of history. Remember how He announced His actions first before actually doing them so that He could prove His reality: *prophecy and then fulfilment* (verses 8-13). In Isaiah's day, more than 100 years before it happened, the LORD clearly predicts the coming of Cyrus, who would defeat Babylon and set the Church free from captivity, allowing them to go back to rebuild Jerusalem.

The fall of Babylon – (47:1-15)

Babylon may not believe these prophecies, but Babylon, like a young queen who has been kept in a cloistered environment, would be taken into captivity in shame and forced to work hard grinding flour (verses 1-3). Yes, the Holy One of Israel may have allowed Babylon to chastise His people (verses 5-6), but only for a short time because Babylon would become very arrogant with her brief taste of power (verses 7-10). In fact, she would see herself as the queen of heaven (verse 7), actually speaking of herself as if she were the LORD God – "I am and there is none besides me" (verses 8 and 10). Babylon would believe that her magicians and occult power is enough to evade all disasters, hide her sins from the LORD and terrorise the world (verses 11-15). The stargazers who make their monthly predictions cannot save Babylon because the fire will burn them up (verse 14).

Israel and Babylon – (48:1-22)

If Babylon is more than simply that one historical empire, but also represents the whole world in its rebellion against the Living God, then Isaiah's prophecy has power for every generation all over the world.

In whatever way the LORD uses us, we can never allow our pride to challenge the glory of Christ and if we look for security anywhere else than in Him, we are doomed to destruction. The Bible ends with Revelation chapters 17-19 declaring to us that Babylon must fall, all over the world, once and for all. We cannot afford to be part of it when its fall does come. We dare not depend on our gods and idols. We must acknowledge the reality of Christ the LORD alone or else we will be destroyed with Babylon.

That is the theme of Isaiah 48.

The people of Israel and Judah may be called by the LORD's name and they may claim to be citizens of the heavenly city (verses 1-2) and they may even claim to trust in Christ, but they are stubborn and stiff-necked (verse 4). The LORD had to predict His actions first before they happened so that when it all happened just as described it would be very clear that none of the idols had done this nor had any human skill or wisdom (verses 3-6). The LORD's prediction of Cyrus was not known before: it is a new prophecy and has never been known before (verses 6-8). It is vital that the sinful people acknowledge this so that the lesson might be learned. The LORD will wait, holding back His wrath, so that enough time could elapse between His prophecy and its fulfilment (verses 9-11).

In fact the LORD waited for around 150 years between giving these detailed prophecies and Cyrus' defeat of Babylon in 539BC.

Christ pleads with His people that they would acknowledge all He has said and done (verses 12-15). He created both the heavens and the earth, standing both at the beginning of history and its end. It might sound unbelievable to the Church of Isaiah's day but not only will Babylon rise to power and take Israel captive, but Babylon will in turn be defeated by the man named Cyrus who the LORD has appointed for the mission.

How can Christ guarantee this? By what authority can He make such claims about history? How can He bring this about? Isaiah 48:16 is

Isaiah

perhaps the greatest Trinitarian verse in the whole Bible. *Christ declares that the Sovereign LORD has sent Him, filled with His Spirit.* Not only are all three members of the Trinity acting together as One God in this verse, but each of them are clearly and simply fulfilling their distinctive role within the Trinity. All the actions of the Living God are *from* the Father, *through* the Son and *in the power* of the Spirit.[74]

Sent from the Father and empowered by the Spirit, Christ is the Redeemer and Holy One of Israel, ready to teach and guide His people (verse 17). If they had listened to Him then they would have known great peace and the Church would have grown far bigger (verses 18-19).

If they are faithful to Him then they must repent and turn away from their stubborn ways (48:4) and never become part of Babylon (verse 20). When it was time to leave Egypt in the Exodus, the people had to eat unleavened bread to show that they were ready to leave quickly (Exodus 12:39). So now they had to be ready to leave Babylon, never looking back like Lot's wife, because the LORD will give them an Exodus experience when He brings them back from exile (verses 20-21).

The wicked, the world of Babylon, will never know the peace that the Church knows in Christ (verse 22).

---

[74] For some unknown reason some Bible translations take the end of verse 16 out of quotation marks as if Isaiah himself suddenly interjects with a statement about himself!

Study 7 Bible Questions

Isaiah 46:1-13

1. Verses 1-2. If Bel and Nebo were ancient Babylonian gods it seems strange that their worshippers had to carry them (their statues) about on ox drawn carts. Why does Isaiah make such a point about these gods being a burden for weary people?

2. What are the man-made gods in your experience that also require so much support and maintenance? Meditate on entertainment systems that need upgrades and have to be carted away to the tip when they fail or our cars which break down or our houses that need huge amounts of money and effort to support. Are there other things that capture our worship or promise us contentment or fulfilment, things that cost us so much?

3. Verses 3-4. List the contrasts between the pagan and man-made gods on the one hand and the LORD God on the other. Notice how Isaiah emphasises how the LORD carries His people.

4. Verse 5-7. What are the main faults with the man-made idols and the false gods?

5. Verses 8-9. What does the Living God want His people to remember?

6. Verses 10-11. What is the main proof that the LORD God provides that He is the only One who can be trusted?

7. Verses 12-13. What is the central promise of the Living God? If we are "far from righteousness" then what is His remedy?

8. Think about conversations we may have had about "the existence of God". Have they been like these words from Isaiah? What should we have done? Did we ever speak about Jesus? Is it possible to speak about the existence of God without talking about Jesus?

Isaiah

Study 7 Further Questions

1. Notice the character of Jesus in Isaiah 42:2-3. One of the big debates in Church history concerned whether we need to make people feel the guilt and seriousness of their sin, through our preaching of the Law, *before* we later preach the comfort of the gospel. Does life already bruise us and snuff us out so that we need comfort and support from Christ? Or does Christ first bruise us and snuff us out before He later comforts us?

2. If Isaiah were writing his critique of idolatry today would he direct it against the Hindu temple, the sports stadia, the mosque, the expensive Church building or the shopping centres? Is the modern atheist an idolater? If we worship an abstract concept of god that is not like Jesus, created with our own traditions or philosophies, could we call this idolatry?

Study 7 Daily Readings

Day 1	Isaiah 42:1-25
Day 2	Isaiah 43:1-28
Day 3	Isaiah 44:1-28
Day 4	Isaiah 45:1-25
Day 5	Isaiah 46:1-13
Day 6	Isaiah 47:1-15
Day 7	Isaiah 48:1-22

The daily Bible readings are an opportunity to not only read through all of the material in the book under study, but also to read parts of the Bible that relate to the themes and issues that we have been considering. Wetry to make sure that we receive light from the whole Bible as we think through the key issues each week.

Swept away

Isaiah

Study 8   The Glory of the Cross: Isaiah 49:1-53:12

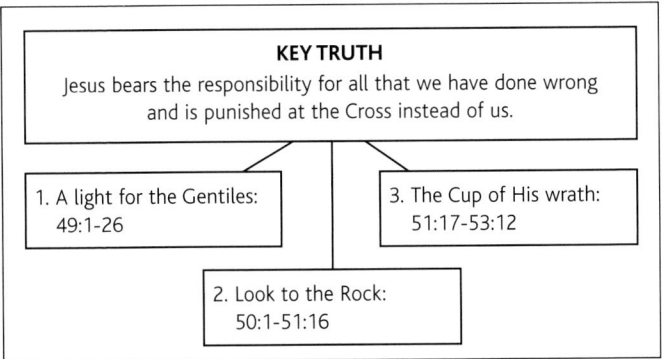

1. *A light for the Gentiles* – 49:1-26

We need a big enough canvas if we are going to see the death of the Divine Servant properly. The death of Jesus Christ the LORD, prophesied from the beginning of the world, determines the destiny of the whole world in every continent in every age. Yes, Jesus of Nazareth died in a corner of the Roman empire, embroiled in the religion and politics of first century Palestine. Yet, to view His death only in this way is to miss the real facts, the global and cosmic nature of His death. The death of Christ the LORD has relevance not only to all the nations of the world but also to the entire heavens and the earth.

In these chapters Christ is set before our eyes in such bright and vivid terms.

> "After having treated of the future deliverance of the people, he comes down to Christ, under whose guidance the people were brought out of Babylon, as they had formerly been brought out of Egypt. The former prophecy must have been confirmed by this doctrine; because they would scarcely have hoped that the Lord would deliver them, if they had not placed Christ before their eyes, by whom alone desponding souls can be comforted and strengthened" (Calvin, commenting on Isaiah 49:1).

Christ was spoken of before His human birth, as we saw in chapters 7-9 and "from the womb He has remembered" His name.

> "The great author and publisher of the redemption produces His authority from heaven for the work He had undertaken. God had appointed Him and set Him apart for it: 'The Lord has called me from the womb to this office and made mention of my name, nominated me to be the Saviour.' By an angel He called him Jesus—a Saviour, who should save his people from their sins, Matt. i. 21. Nay, from the womb of the divine counsels, before all worlds, He was called to this service" (Matthew Henry).

Christ, as the very Word of God, has that sword coming from His mouth (verse 2) as John describes in Revelation 19:15 (see also Hebrews 4:12). He is the arrow that will accomplish all that the Father requires, His faithful Servant. Jesus does everything that the Father does (John 5:19) and the Father does all His work through Christ. Yet, His work has met with constant opposition and His own people have consistently failed to trust Him and have sinned so badly against Him.

John 1:10-11 summarises the Bible's whole story of Christ's discouragements in His work – "He was in the world, and though the world was made through Him, the world did not recognise Him. He came to His own people, but His own people did not receive Him."

Yet, Christ always entrusts Himself to His Father's will (49:4b). The Father has sent Him to bring Jacob/Israel to Himself – to redeem the Church (verse 5). Christ has great honour from the Father so the Father tells Him that it is too small a mission to bring only the people of Israel to Him. The Father will also make Christ a light to all the nations of the world (49:6) – "that my salvation may reach to the ends of the earth". Yes, Christ may be despised and rejected by His own people, so the Gentile kings and rulers all over the world will acknowledge Him and worship Him as the Chosen One of God (verse 7).

Christ is Himself the covenant for the people (verse 8), guiding, protecting and caring for the Church from all over the world (verses 8-11). The whole universe, the heavens and the earth, rejoices in this global redemption because this was the very purpose of creation.

Isaiah

Yes, that sounds wonderful and glorious, but isn't it too good to be true? The Church suffers so many persecutions. We are rejected and hated; we suffer the same illnesses and afflictions as everyone else. Surely the LORD has forgotten us (verse 14). But, even though a mother may in extreme circumstances forget her own baby, yet the LORD God could never forget His Church (verse 15). He has engraved the Church onto the palms of His hands (verse 16).

> "*Behold* is a word intended to excite admiration. Here, indeed, we have a theme for marvelling. Heaven and earth may well be astonished that rebels should obtain so great a nearness to the heart of infinite love as to be written upon the palms of His hands. "I have graven *thee.*" *It* does not say, "Thy name." The name is there, but that is not all: "I have graven thee." See the fulness of this! I have graven thy person, thine image, thy case, thy circumstances, thy sins, thy temptations, thy weaknesses, thy wants, thy works; I have graven thee, everything about thee, all that concerns thee; I have put thee altogether there. Wilt thou ever say again that thy God hath forsaken thee when He has graven thee upon His own palms?" (Spurgeon's devotional on Isaiah 49:16).[75]

Though Israel was sent into exile and must have felt as if there was no future for her, yet not only was she going to be restored, but looking further ahead she would expand far beyond anything she could imagine. Prophesying the time when Israel would go out to the whole world, bursting out of the small boundaries of that little land (verse 19), the LORD promises a day when she would be amazed at all her children – "where have they come from?" (verse 21).

The answer is that the Sovereign LORD Himself has gathered them, bringing them in from every nation (verse 22). Rulers from nations all over the world will bow down to join the Church as they hope in Christ (verses 22-23). Those that persecute the Church will be persecuted by Christ Himself – verse 25 (see also 2 Thesssalonians 1:6).

---

75 We might also say that given the manner of His death, by crucifixion, His palms have been so completely committed to us. The nail prints, the wounds that He still retains as marks of His glory, are the most powerful statement of His love for us.

The global mission of Christ reaches its climax in verse 26 – "then the whole human race will know that I, the LORD, am your Saviour, your Redeemer, the Mighty One of Jacob."

2. *Look to the Rock* – 50:1-51:16

The obedient Servant (50:1-11)

Israel realised that her sin was great and feared that the situation had gone too far, that the marriage was over – that the bill of divorce had been issued (verse 1). Yes, her sins had broken the relationship, but it was broken on her side not His (verse 2). Why did Israel give up on Him so easily? Why assume that He could not save or heal? (Verse 2).

> "In creation is demonstrated, in particular, his power to effect dramatic changes: the sea dries; rivers become desert; the sky goes from light to darkness. Can such a God not equally transform the fortunes of His people He dried up the Red Sea (Exodus 14; he turned the Nile to blood and its fish stank (Exodus 7:17-18); he visited Egypt with palpable darkness (Exodus 10:21) but gave his people light (Exodus 10:23)" (Motyer, 398).

So, from verse 4-11 Christ the Divine Servant speaks about how He is able to save His people from their sins. His Father has sent Him to speak His word. He speaks nothing of His own but only what the Father tells Him to say (John 8:28 and John 12:49 – "For I did not speak of my own accord, but the Father who sent me commanded me what to say and how to say it."). Unlike Israel, Christ is always obedient to His Father (50:5). In verse 6 we have a prophecy of how He would be treated just before His crucifixion (see Matthew 26:67; 27:26-31). Yet, even though Christ would receive such cruel abuse in obedience to His Father, yet He trusts in His Father to vindicate Him in the end (verses 7-8). No one has anything to accuse Him of (50:8-9), so only false accusations were offered when they did kill Him (see Matthew 26:59-60).

The key application is in verses 10-11. If we are in darkness, if our sins have overwhelmed us, what are we going to do? We could try to make our own torches and save ourselves (verse 11), but then we will die in torment. So, instead, we must fear the LORD and obey the word of His

Isaiah

Servant (verse 10). We must not despair in our sin, but continue to trust our Saviour. The Servant can save us.

Look to the Rock – (51:1-16)

We must trust Christ to save us, just as Abraham did long ago. We need to go back to learn from Abraham, the father of the faith; the rock from which all his children have been quarried. A child of Abraham is not defined by genealogy or genetics, but by trusting in Christ the LORD. That is what Jesus Himself said in John 8 and the apostle Paul spells it out in Romans 9. Christ the LORD can certainly restore Zion, but she must trust Him. He can restore the world back to the garden of the LORD (verse 3), bringing joy and gladness to His people.

He will do this not just for His ancient people who face exile in Babylon, but for all the nations of the world (verses 4-5). Think of the whole universe, the heavens and the earth. They seem so big and permanent, yet they will wear out in the end. However, the salvation that Christ will achieve lasts forever, on a scale beyond even the whole universe as we know it (verse 6). When the wicked attack the followers of Christ, they simply need to remember this big perspective (verses 7-8). The wicked have no future at all, other than the grave, whereas the LORD's salvation opens up an everlasting future with Him.

In this chapter Christ has the title of "The Arm of the LORD" (see verses 5 and 9).[76] Just as He destroyed Egypt (Rahab – see Isaiah 30:7) and took His people through the Red Sea to the Promised Land (verses 9-10), so He will restore Israel again (verse 11). First, He will bring them back from the exile of Babylon, but ultimately He will bring about this complete renewal of the whole creation so that death and sorrow will be gone forever, "will flee away" (verse 11).

How can the Church ever fear mere human beings when the Living God, who made all things, is with her? (Verses 12-13). Whatever she is going

---

[76] "1). It was the LORD himself who went out to Egypt to save his people (Ex. 3:1-8); he did so by his outstretched arm (Deut 4:34 etc). 2). Isaiah personified the Lord's Arm (51:9) and foresaw the Lord exposing his Arm in the work of salvation (52:10). 3) Consequently in 53:1 the 'Arm' is the LORD himself come to save, revealed in the following verses as a true Man among men... and we know that this Arm of the LORD is Jesus" (Motyer).

through right now, whether imprisonment or hunger, He will soon put everything right. If He was able to set the heavens in place and found the earth, then He can certainly come to the aid of His people (verses 14-16).

3. *The Cup of His wrath* – 51:17-53:12

The cup of His wrath – (51:17-23)

So, though Israel may feel that she has suffered the wrath of the LORD God, draining the cup of His wrath to the bottom (5:17-20), yet that cup of wrath will be taken from her (verse 22). The wrath of God will fall on the enemies of the Church rather than the Church herself (verse 23).

Furthermore, Christ Himself will drink that cup for the Church – as we will see from the end of chapter 52 and into 53. The wicked must bear the wrath of God for themselves, but Christ will bear it *on behalf of* the Church, so that her sins may be forgiven and her problems healed.

The feet of gospel preachers – (52:1-12)

Isaiah could see hard times ahead for the Church ending with a terrible conquest by the Babylonians and exile. Yet, when they were in exile in Babylon they needed to keep a firm trust in the Promised Christ and remain full of joy and strength (52:1). Though a captive (verse 2), Jerusalem needed to trust her future to Christ.

Just as she was enslaved for no payment, so He will set her free for no payment (verse 3). He saved her from both Egypt through Moses and Assyria under Hezekiah, and now He would save her from the Babylonians who blaspheme His name (verses 4-5).

It is wonderful to hear the gospel (the good news) when we are feeling so low, to hear that our God reigns (verse 7). He imagines watchmen who catch sight of the exiles returning accompanied by the LORD and all the celebrations this will produce (verses 8-9). The nations of the world will once again be drawn to Christ through His saving action in plain historical view (verse 10).

So, if the Church will not always be in exile in Babylon, that must effect how they deal with Babylon in the here and now. As pagan Babylon blasphemes the LORD, yet the Church in exile will have nothing to do

Isaiah

with that (verse 11). She will keep herself pure from such uncleanness so that when it is time to leave she will leave with dignity in the glorious presence of the God of Israel (verses 11-12). In 2 Corinthians 6:17 the apostle Paul reminds us of this prophecy, when he teaches us not to join up with unbelievers. We are still the Church in exile awaiting our return to Zion, so we too need to remain pure and faithful to Christ the LORD.

The suffering and glory of Christ – (52:13-53:12)

This next prophecy of Isaiah is perhaps the most famous because it so accurately and powerfully describes the sufferings of the LORD Jesus Christ on the Cross. Perhaps only Psalm 22 can equal this prophecy of the Cross. Whenever Isaiah assures the Church of the salvation that Christ will work for her, he always then goes on to describe more about Christ the Servant of the LORD and His work.

So, having lost all the outward signs of the gospel in captive exile in Babylon, what did the ancient Church need to think about? What should fill their hearts and minds? We too, as we wait in exile here, how can we know for sure that our day of restoration and redemption will come?

"See, my Servant…", says God the Father. Look to Christ and we will have all the joy, confidence and strength that we need. Christ will always act wisely, even when He is under the most terrible pressure and persecution (52:13). The strange paradox is that "He will be raised and lifted up": both mean that He will be glorified but also that He will be crucified.

Jesus Himself quotes from Isaiah 52:13 just before John quotes 53:1 to explain the reaction of people to Him. John 12:32-33 – "'I, when I am lifted up from the earth, will draw all people to myself.' He said this to show the kind of death He was going to die" (see also John 3:14; 8:28).

As Jesus said, even when He is lifted up and so disfigured by His suffering and abuse that the crowds are appalled at Him, it is at that very time that He will draw all people to Himself – "he will sprinkle many nations." Even the ignorant Gentiles will see and understand in the light of the Cross (52:15).

Yet, not everyone will respond to the Suffering Servant, Crucified Christ. That is precisely the point that John makes when reminding us of this prophecy from Isaiah. There was nothing about Jesus in terms of outward appearance that would make people love Him so those who judge by the flesh would have no interest in Him (53:1-2).

> John 12:37-41 – "Even after Jesus had done all these miraculous signs in their presence, they still would not believe in Him. This was to fulfill the word of Isaiah the prophet: "Lord, who has believed our message and to whom has the arm of the Lord been revealed?" For this reason they could not believe, because, as Isaiah says elsewhere: "He has blinded their eyes and deadened their hearts, so they can neither see with their eyes, nor understand with their hearts, nor turn — and I would heal them." Isaiah said this because he saw Jesus' glory and spoke about Him."

It seems incredible that as the LORD of Glory, the First and the Last, who defeated 185,000 Assyrian soldiers in one night, He should be "a Man of suffering and familiar with pain" (53:3). Yet, how wonderful it is that in our own deep pain and suffering we know that the King of Kings, the Ruler of the universe has been there before us. He is a High Priest who fully sympathises with us.

What a terrible indictment of the human race that when the LORD of Glory was among us "He was despised and we held Him in low esteem" (53:3). Is not this the very worst crime we have ever committed? We know how to feel outrage about crimes against humanity but what do we care about crimes against deity?

He went through this in order to save us. Even while we turned against Him – and this is what all sin really is – He was suffering and dying in order that we do not need to (53:4).

As Charles Wesley so brilliantly expressed it – "O Jesus my hope, for me offered up, Who with clamour pursued Thee to Calvary's top, The blood Thou hast shed, for me let it plead, And declare Thou hast died in Thy murderer's stead."

At the Cross the crowds assumed that Jesus was being punished for His own sins (53:4), yet He was actually being punished for our sins! The Lamb was being sacrificed in our place, just as the sacrificial lambs had been sacrificed for so many centuries.

Isaiah

Although some people get very confused about why Jesus had to die, Isaiah explains it so well. He is the spotless sacrificial lamb but we are the sinful, rebellious sheep. We are all like wandering sheep going our own way (53:6), so the LORD actually puts the blame for all our iniquity onto Jesus.[77] He bears the responsibility for all that we have done wrong and is punished at the Cross instead of us.

As we have seen over and over again through the Book of Isaiah, the judgment of the Living God will fall on the earth and nobody can survive that day of punishment, cleansing and renewal. When He comes to get rid of all the wickedness, injustice and uncleanness in the world, there is no place for any of us sinful people. Isaiah has described in plain terms how the LORD will break, crush, burn, consume, destroy and forget the wicked on His day of vengeance – (consider Isaiah 1:28 and 31; 2:8-11, 19-21; 3:8-9; 5:14-15, 20-25; 6:11-13; 9:18-20; 10:1-4; 24:1-5, 17-23; 26:14, 21; 30:27-28, 33; 34:1-10; 37:36; 44:10-11; 47:14-15; 49:26; 63:1-6; 65:11-12; 66:4, 15-16, 24). The rest of the prophets and Moses say the same thing. Sin cuts us off from the LORD God, from His life and peace and safety (see Isaiah 59:2).

The Servant of the LORD is the Holy One of Israel, the only One who has nothing to fear from the day of judgment. Yet, He allowed Himself to be led like a lamb to sacrifice (53:7) so that He could take our place under that judgment of the Living God. He allowed Himself to be cut off from the living (the punishment for sin that was described at the very beginning in Genesis 2:17). He was cut off so that we never need to be (53:8). Though He had never done anything wrong, yet He was given to death and buried like a criminal with the wicked and rich (53:9).[78]

Could this all have been some terrible mistake, some dreadful tragedy? No, *it was actually the LORD's will to do this*. All through the book of Isaiah Christ has promised that He would be able to save His people from the day of judgment and this is the only way that it could be done. The LORD Himself makes Jesus an "offering for sin" (53:10). Here Isaiah speaks of the guilt offering of Leviticus 5:14-19. It covers offences against both the

---

77 "The substitutionary imagery of verse 6c is drawn straight from Leviticus 16" (Motyer, 429).

78 Jesus was of course buried in a rich man's grave as we read in Matthew 27:57-61. However, notice how the wicked and the rich are considered to be the same thing.

LORD and other human beings, whether there was any intention or not – "If anyone sins and does what is forbidden in any of the LORD's commands, even though they do not know it, they are guilty and held responsible" (Leviticus 5:17). All the Gentile nations that would be drawn to Christ by His death knew nothing of His laws or character, yet they too are guilty of sin. Christ's death covers their sin. In addition the guilt offering of Leviticus 5 must also be accompanied by a restitution, more than making up for what has been lost through the sin. This is why the righteousness of Christ is so strongly emphasised by Isaiah. His death not only takes away the sin but His perfect life that is such a delight to His Father (42:1) perfects the true and perfect atonement for our sin.

Yet, His death is not the end of Him because He will be brought back to life and see the fruit of His work (53:11). Verse 11 speaks of the knowledge of Christ the LORD: He knows all about the needs of the situation and how they are to be answered.[79] Perhaps the best way to translate the verse is something like, "by His knowledge that Righteous One, my Servant, will provide righteousness for many." Christ the LORD knows what is needed and He is Himself appointed as 'the Servant' to answer those needs. He is personally Righteous and therefore is not only faultless in all He does but also is a totally acceptable sacrificial lamb, without spot or blemish. He is the Righteous One but He so identifies Himself with the 'many' that they receive His righteousness and He takes on their sinfulness.

> Isaiah 53:11 is one of the fullest statements of atonement theology ever penned. (i) The Servant knows the needs to be met and what must be done. (ii) As 'that righteous one, my servant' he is both fully acceptable to the God our sins have offended and has been appointed by him to his task. (iii) As righteous, he is free from every contagion of our sin. (iv) He identified himself personally with our sin and need. (v) The emphatic pronoun 'he' underlines his personal commitment to this role. (vi) He accomplishes the task fully. Negatively, in the bearing of iniquity; positively, in the provision of righteousness. (Motyer, 442)

---

[79] It is possible to take 'the knowledge of Him' as meaning 'knowledge about Him' or 'knowing Him' so that the focus is on the way that sinners come to know Him and therefore receive His righteousness. However, it may be better to leave the focus on Christ Himself rather than on the fact that we come to know Him.

Isaiah

Again we might want to consider a better translation of 53:12 – "I will apportion to Him the many and the strong He will apportion as spoil." The 'many' who have receievd His righteousness will be given to Him as His own. He has bought His Church with His own life and now we belong to Him, assigned to Him by God the Father by the solemn eternal covenant. In the same way, by His victory Jesus has taken possession of the whole world and He now can do with the strong as He wishes. All the resources and kingdoms of the world belong to Him.

Having completed this incredible work of redemption through His death and resurrection, Jesus was received into the Highest Heaven as the rightful ruler over the whole universe (53:12). Having been counted as a sinner and having paid for sin, now He lives to make intercession for sinners (see Hebrews 7:25).

Study 8 Bible Questions

Isaiah 51:9-16

1. Verse 9a. This is the first of three calls to "Awake! Awake!": the first is to "the Arm of the LORD"; the second is to Jerusalem and the third is to Zion. What is the difference between these three subjects that are told to "Awake!"? Who is the "Arm of the LORD"?

2. Verses 9-10. The whole section is addressed to "the Arm of the LORD", so what did He do in "generations of old"? What incident from "days gone by" is being remembered here? Who is Rahab? (See Isaiah 30:7).

3. Verse 11. It is as if the people of Judah are already in exile even though the Babylonian exile was still decades into the future. What is the deeper 'exile' that Isaiah is speaking of here? What is the final hope that he is holding up for the Church in every age?

4. Verse 12-13a. Why is it so important to spend time every day thinking about "Our Father in heaven"? Why did Jesus, the Arm of the LORD, have to keep that in mind as He faced His great work on earth?

5. Verse 13. When we are surrounded by all the empires, tyrannies and ideologies of this passing age, how can we be free from fear or "constant terror"?

6. Verse 14. We can easily fall into the view that the sufferings and troubles of this mortal life as the end of the story, as if they had the final word. What is the Biblical remedy for this? Why did this comfort have special power for the Arm of the LORD in His great work?

7. Verse 15. Why is it so important to know that the LORD God has power over the sea?

8. Verse 16. The final words are specially spoken to the Arm of the LORD by His Father in heaven, but they also include Zion, the Church of the Living God – "You are my people". What is the great comfort of this verse?

Isaiah

Study 8   Further Questions

1. One idea is that the death of Jesus was 'for sin' or 'because of sin' in the sense that He was killed by sinful people because they were sinners. He was the victim of their sin, and the LORD God was showing us how to forgive when we are victims of sin. There is an element of truth in this: yes, because we are sinners, we killed Jesus and yes, He was showing us how to behave when evil is done to us (1 Peter 2:20-25, referring to Isaiah 53:9). However, what would Isaiah say is the deep purpose behind the death of Jesus?

2. Why does the Living God punish sin? Is it to balance His cosmic books of justice, making sure that good and evil are properly balanced out in the end? Why can't the LORD God come to terms with evil and simply 'live with it' or 'tolerate it'? Why is He so passionately concerned to not only drive evil out of His good creation but also to see to it that evil gets paid back? Why can't evil simply 'get away with it'?

Study 8   Daily Readings

Day 1	Isaiah 49:1-7
Day 2	Isaiah 49:8-26
Day 3	Isaiah 50:1-11
Day 4	Isaiah 51:1-16
Day 5	Isaiah 51:17-23
Day 6	Isaiah 52:1-12
Day 7	Isaiah 52:13-53:12

The brave new world

Isaiah

Study 9 The Glory of the Gospel: Isaiah 54:1-59:21

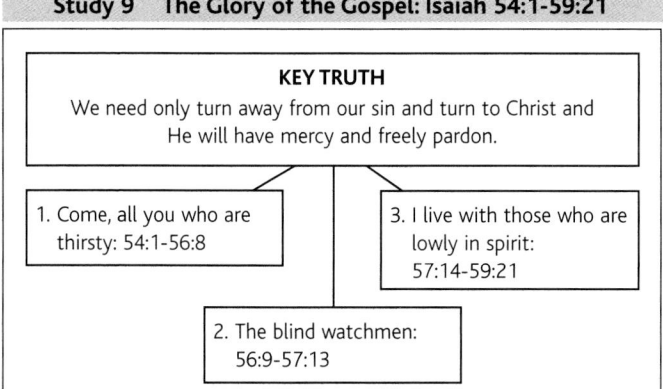

1. *Come, all you who are thirsty* – 54:1-56:8

Marriage restoration (54:1-17)

In Isaiah 50 Israel's sins had threatened a divorce in the marriage covenant between Christ and the Church, but now the marriage is restored and reaffirmed.

> "The barren woman sings, not because she has ceased to be barren but because the Lord has acted in his Servant with the effect that his 'seed' (53:11) become her children/sons. The picture of Sarah, the barren woman who was to bear the miracle child and become the mother of a family more numerous than the stars, provides the background (Genesis 11:30; 16:1; Isaiah 51:2)" (Motyer, 445).

The global expansion of Israel after the death and resurrection of Jesus is clearly in view here (verses 2-3). The times of rebellion and punishment will be forgotten (verse 4) as the Divine Husband, the Holy One of Israel, the Redeemer and God of all the earth, brings her honour. The deserted wife is restored to the family home, full of joy (verse 6). Yes, her sin and adultery had caused a separation (verse 7), but with compassion and

everlasting kindness, He took His anger on Himself. If a husband takes back a wife who has deeply and repetitively betrayed him, then her shame falls onto him: people will think he is stupid to bother with her. Nevertheless, the Divine Husband takes this shame as He welcomes back His wife.

Just as in the days of Noah when He promised never again to flood the earth, so He promises never to pour out His anger on His Church ever again (verses 9-10). Through the sacrifice of the Lamb of God, the crucifixion of Christ, His anger has been taken into His own life, borne upon His own shoulders.

His unfailing love is stronger than the foundations of the earth (verse 10).

Zion may have been shamed and destroyed, but He will build the City of God using the very best resources (verses 11-12). We see that completed and the glorious City of God descending out of heaven to earth on the day of new creation, when Christ returns in glory, in Revelation 21:9-27.

The LORD Himself will teach Zion's children (54:13 – see 1 John 2:20 and 27; John 6:45; Jeremiah 31:31-34). The LORD who rules over all things, including the blacksmith and the destroyer, will make sure that no weapon will kill the Church and no accusation will remain unanswered (54:14-17). The LORD will make sure the Church is safe and vindicated.

Come, all you who are thirsty (55:1-13)

So, if the Church is bound to Christ with an everlasting covenant of love, the whole world may come to find refreshment in Zion. Of course this great feast will be held for all the righteous from every nation in that new creation future (Revelation 19:6-9), but even now as we come to Christ we find in Him the Bread and Water of Life.

John 6:35 – "Jesus declared, "I am the bread of life. He who comes to me will never go hungry, and he who believes in me will never be thirsty." (See also John 4:10-14). In Christ we freely receive all that we need. Our souls are satisfied in Him.

Isaiah

Spurgeon brilliantly preached this prophecy of Isaiah:

> "I will just preach this salvation, for this is the wine and milk which is proclaimed without money and without price. Beloved, all this is to be gained by faith in Christ—whosoever believeth in him who died upon the tree, and groaned away his life for us—shall never come into condemnation: he is passed from death unto life, and the love of God abideth in him. And now, having thus exhibited the article, my next business is to *bring the bidders up to the auction box and sell it*. My difficulty is to bring you *down* to my price, as old Rowland said. He was preaching in a fair, and he heard a man selling his goods. "Ah!" said he, "as for those people over there, their difficulty is to bring people up to their price; whereas, my difficulty is to bring you *down* to my price." Now, here is a gospel fully preached, without money and without price. Here comes some one up to the sacred desk, transformed for the moment into an auction box, and he cries, "I want to buy." What will you give for it? He holds out his hands, and he has such a handful; he has to lift up his very lap with more, for he can hardly hold all his good works… "I am very attentive to my prayers I go to Church almost as soon as the doors are open… and I attend the prayer-meetings and beside that, I pay everybody twenty shillings in the pound. I had rather pay twenty-one shillings than nineteen. I would not like to hurt anybody. I do not tread upon a worm if I can help it, I am always liberal, and assist the poor when I can"… I will send you away; there is no salvation for you, for it is "without money and without price;" and as long as you bring these fine good works of yours you cannot have it… Our hope must be built on nothing less than Jesus' blood and righteousness, and when we have built a foundation with that, we may have as many good works as we like—the more the better. But for a foundation, good works are fickle and feeble things, and he that useth them will see his house totter to the ground."

The promises of Christ given to David are an everlasting covenant (verse 3). Christ is not just for some, but for all (verse 5) and people from all over the world will come running to buy from Christ.

Now He is available. Now Christ is on offer (verse 6). If we seek Him now we will certainly find Him, because He has solemnly made that promise to us (Matthew 7:7).

Is He hard to find? Is it really possible to buy the Bread and Water and Wine and Milk of eternal life from Christ for free? Yes, 55:7, we need only turn *away* from our sin and turn *to* Christ and He will have mercy and freely pardon.

This doesn't make sense to us. We are so used to mere religion and self-improvement. Our hearts are used to hiding in the darkness, hiding away from the Living God. We find it hard to understand this free love and grace of the LORD God. Yes, His thoughts are as high above us as the heavens are above the earth (55:9). Even our best thoughts about God are lost in impersonal, philosophical abstractions, whereas the Father, Son and Spirit cannot be contained by our little ways of thinking.

His word goes out of His mouth to produce a fruitful harvest (55:10-11). So what does His word promise for us? That we will go out with great joy and peace, and that the whole creation will burst into song with us as the thorns that have cursed the earth since Genesis 3:17-19 are gone forever! It sounds too marvellous to be true and yet His word always accomplishes what He wills.

Eunuchs and Foreigners – (56:1-8)

So, if the Church is open for business, ready to receive people from all over the world to buy the free refreshment of Christ, who is invited? Surely the pagans and those excluded by the Law are not invited to Christ's resurrection feast?

The chapter begins by reminding all those thirsty people who have come and called on the LORD (55:1 and 6) how to live as the Church of God. If the resurrection future, the home of righteousness, is going to be revealed so soon, then we are to live out that righteousness here and now (56:1). The issue of the Sabbath is chosen as the key example of this.

Isaiah has already warned about keeping Sabbath in a merely religious way (1:13), but here he is thinking of Sabbath as the glorious presentation of the free forgiveness that is in Christ. Sabbath is about

Isaiah

rest: it is about ceasing from our labours (Hebrews 4:10). We keep the Sabbath when we turn away from our sin and trust entirely in Christ the LORD.

So, what about those that the Law excludes from the presence of the LORD: the eunuchs and the Gentiles?

Neither the Gentiles nor the eunuchs must think themselves excluded (56:3). The eunuchs who keep the LORD's Sabbath and hold fast to His gospel covenant, will be welcome within His temple, with a better heritage than any number of children (56:4-5). The Gentiles who are bound to Christ and eager to serve Him will be brought onto the LORD's holy mountain and welcome to offer sacrifices in the temple.

The LORD's temple is a house of prayer *for all nations*.

This is such a shocking prophecy. The purpose of the Law about eunuchs and Gentiles had been misunderstood and applied in a legalistic way, becoming a barrier blocking such people from coming into the temple and coming to Christ the LORD. The Sovereign LORD gathers the exiles of Israel not only from Israel and Judah but also from all the other nations too (56:8).

When Jesus came to the temple in Matthew 21:12-17 He quoted this very Scripture. They had developed money changing practices to exclude not just Gentile people but even Gentile money from within the temple! So, He immediately invited the physically disabled people, who would normally be banned from the temple, right into the temple where He healed them. Notice that He did not heal them first and then allow them in, but invited them into His temple even while they were still physically broken.

2. *The blind watchmen* – 56:9-57:13

Israel's leaders are supposed to be on the lookout, watching carefully over the sheep, the flock of God's Church. They should be protecting the flock from the false teachers, the pagan infiltration and the compromised lifestyles. They should be given loving and firm pastoral care so that the LORD's people, will be properly discipled. If the Gentiles are coming in from all over the world, these leaders need to be fully alert and ready to serve them.

Yet, they are actually blind and ignorant (56:10). All the wild beasts, the lions and wolves and dogs feel free to wander into the sheepfold because the shepherds won't do anything to stop them (verse 9). The shepherds are pleasing themselves, seeking their own pleasure while getting drunk (verses 11-12).

These selfish leaders assume that the future is smooth and full of pleasure (56:12). Yet, living a long life full of pleasure may not be the best life to have. It is better to die early if it will spare us from falling into sin (57:1). We are challenged to consider how the LORD allows the righteous to die for their own good. This is not the sort of thing we often think about, yet it helps us to understand the way that the LORD deals with His people.

> "God gathers them, and places them in safety from being distressed by prevailing afflictions. The general meaning is, that wicked men grievously deceive themselves by supposing that there is no greater happiness than to have life continued to a great age, and by thus pluming themselves on their superiority to the servants of God, who die early. Being attached to the world, they likewise harden themselves by this pretence, that... while others die, they continue to be safe and sound" (Calvin).[80]

Instead of pretending that their long life and pleasure is a sign of God's favour, the arrogant and mocking sinners need to carefully consider their lives (verses 3-5). They were brought up in unfaithful families (verse 3) and they have carried on with the same behaviour, mocking and sneering at the righteous (verse 4). They even commit immorality in pagan activities and sacrifice their children by throwing them into the ravines (verse 5). Perhaps the children were interfering in their pursuit of pleasure or their plans for their lives so they chose to get rid of them. The pagan

---

80 Calvin goes on to say, "In our own times a remarkable instance of this was given in the death of Luther, who was snatched from the world a short time before that terrible calamity befell Germany, which he had foretold many years before, when he exclaimed loudly against that contempt of the Gospel, and that wickedness and licentiousness which everywhere prevailed. Frequently had he entreated the Lord to call him out of this life before he beheld that dreadful punishment, the anticipation of which filled him with trembling and horror. And he obtained it from the Lord. Soon after his death, lo, a sudden and unforeseen war sprang up, by which Germany was terribly afflicted, when nothing was farther from her thoughts than the dread of such a calamity."

Isaiah

religions were full of sinful pleasures and self indulgence. We can well imagine that such pagan activities were the height of fashion and all the "best" people indulged. What harm could it do to have one of the latest designs of pagan symbols behind your door (verse 8)?

While they committed sexual sins, the LORD knew they were forsaking Him and committing adultery against Him (57:8). Verse 9 is misleading in the NIV translation. This verse literally says "you went to the king" (Hebrew *melek*, not the pagan god *Molech*). The pact with death here is the same thing that Isaiah mentioned in 28:14-15 when they went down to Egypt to make a political alliance.[81]

Out of fear (57:11) they went about with great energy to make these political alliances (57:10), but the real problem is that they did not fear Christ the LORD (end of verse 11). The idols of money, pleasure, sex and political alliances would not save them when the time arrives, but whoever takes refuge in Christ will have a resurrection future in the new creation and a home in the City of God (verse 13).

3. *I live with those who are lowly in spirit* – 57:14-59:21

I live with the lowly – (57:14-21)

The LORD's people may have sinned against Him and they carry on sinning against Him (see verse 17), yet the High and Exalted One will actually live with those who are sorry for their sin and have a humble spirit (verse 15). It is one of the greatest promises in the whole Bible. The Living God is high and exalted, always beyond the limited and clumsy ideas of merely human thinking and life, so glorious that to even see Him is to die. Even the highest heaven is too small and limited for the Trinity to dwell, yet anyone who calls out to Christ in humility and repentance will know the indwelling Trinity!

---

81 "The background to this reference is chapters 7 and 28-35, the periods of the disastrous flirtings with Assyria and Egypt respectively. In 28:14-15 Isaiah used the Sheol metaphor to expose the politicians who came back waving their piece of paper and crowing about 'peace in our time' – they had only signed the national death warrant! It is the same here. This is not an attempt to enrol the assistance of supernatural powers but a straight reminder that when the people of God seek strength and security in and through the world all they achieve is death" (Motyer, 474).

Our Father in heaven sees our sin, feels His anger against our sin and hides His face from us, yet because of Christ's death His anger can be turned away and He will turn towards us in love and peace. He will come near to us not to destroy and punish but to heal and restore (verses 16-18). Those that are mourning – as opposed to the foolish, mocking 'fun' of 56:12 – will find that the LORD creates praise on their lips (verse 19a). The wicked may get caught up in giddy celebrations right now (56:9-12; 57:3-10), but they are lost in the restless chaos of the sea. The wicked will never find that Sabbath rest (cf 48:22; 56:1-8) that the eunuchs and Gentiles find when they come to Christ.

True Fasting – (58:1-14)

Isaiah has challenged the people to come back to the LORD God with sincerity and brokenness. The contrite and lowly will be the dwelling place of the Majestic God! So, it seems that there had been perhaps times of national fasting and days when the people were encouraged to come near to God. Yet Isaiah could see that many if not most of the people were only doing this on the surface but in their hearts they were still far from the LORD God (Isaiah 29:13).

Isaiah unmasks the true nature of their fasting, declaring the persistent sin and rebellion that lurks behind the masks (verse 1). On the surface all looked very encouraging with an apparent eagerness to do what is right (verse 2), but the attitude is all wrong (verse 3). The people feel that their fasting should have 'earned' a response from the LORD, as if they now deserved a mighty miracle of blessing (verse 3).

This attitude is all too common when Christians fast in every age. The sinful feeling quickly enters in that we are doing God a favour by fasting – whereas the real purpose of fasting is to change our own hearts, to teach us that more than any food we need Christ, the Word of God.

Isaiah was not looking at the missed meals but at the sinful behaviour that was still going on even with grumbling, empty stomachs (verses 3-5). How can their voice be heard in heaven when they keep on with the greed and strife yet outwardly bow their heads, putting on sackcloth and pretending to be lowly?

If that is what they think of as a 'fast' then it is no wonder that the LORD is not interested.

Isaiah

The kind of fast that the LORD requires finds its centre not in the lack of food but in the plenty of righteousness (verses 6-7).

The lack of food is supposed to remind us and spur us on to live like Christ: setting people free from injustice; breaking the chains that enslave people; overthrowing oppression.[82] If we are not eating food on our fast then it is a good opportunity to give our food (or the money we have saved) to those who are hungry and needy (verse 7). When this kind of fasting happens then the glory of Christ will shine on us and our true healing will quickly begin (verse 8). If we are lowly and contrite in this way, then the LORD in His high and holy place (57:15) will hear and come to dwell with us (verse 9), giving us the help that we need.

The true sign of repentance is when we stop doing our sin and start doing what is right; when we have really turned away from the old life and put on Christ (verses 9-10). The "pointing finger and the malicious talk" is always the first place to look. It is so natural to us to accuse others and speak badly of each other. When the repentance has reached that place then we know that it is for real.

Then refreshment in the desert and restoration of Zion can begin (verses 11-12). Returning to the Sabbath theme from chapter 56, Isaiah explains how the Sabbath is about more than refraining from normal work. Sabbath is when we find rest from our sin; rest from our own way and our own selfish desires; rest from speaking wrong or foolish words (58:13-14). When we delight in finding rest in the LORD, honouring Him with the day, then we will know His joy and blessing.

No-one is righteous (59:1-21)

Yes, the LORD can save us even when we feel that it is too late or we are too bad (59:1), but we must recognise how serious our sins really are (59:2). The things we have done wrong and all that we have failed to do right cuts us off from the Holy and Majestic Living God. Sin is everything that He hates and He cannot even look at us in our sin (verse 2).

---

82 There are so many ways that Christians can get involved in this locally, nationally and internationally. However, perhaps it is always best to start with our own life and local setting. Am I oppressing people in my own life, through my employment practices or the way I treat others? Then, what is going on in my local village or town? How is my local Church involved, for good or ill? Who is enslaved, by drugs, alcohol, debt, prostitution, illness, depression etc? Do people think first of our local Church when they need help?

Sin clings to us, covering us with its pollution (59:3) and we cannot wash it off ourselves.

Sin ruins us so that nobody really cares about the kind of justice that the LORD desires. Instead our words become empty and we actually produce even more evil (verse 4). We are like snakes laying eggs filled with poisonous snakes or like spiders trying to make clothes of righteousness out of mere cobwebs. Our actions leave a poisonous legacy and our good deeds are so useless that they can never cover us up (verses 5-6). In fact our actions are evil and we love violence. We might pretend to hate violence, but look at our entertainment – the games we play and the films we watch. Listen to the violence in our words.

Far from running away from sin, we actually run towards it. Yes, our hearts are filled with sinful desires and we are attracted to it, even if it means innocent people get hurt (verse 7).[83] Verse 8 reminds us that the wicked can never know peace and their lives will always be mixed up and complicated. The apostle Paul quotes these verses in Romans 3:15-17 when he wants to show that we are all sinful and condemned.

As long as we walk along that path we will never know that peace and joy that comes when the High and Exalted LORD God dwells with us. We will grope around in darkness, not knowing what to do with our lives or where to go (verses 9-10). We may moan a lot (verse 11), but we cannot find real justice or rescue if we will not come to the Righteous Redeemer.

Notice how Isaiah *began* speaking to other people (verses 1-8), but now he includes himself (verses 9-15).

We need to face up to our situation as it really is with no more pretence (verses 12-15). Our sins, offences and iniquities are all heaped up and always with us (verse 12).[84] Rebellion and treachery, turning our backs on

---

83 This can happen in all kinds of ways. Whenever we look at porn we oppress the people who get so damaged by a cruel and exploitative industry. Who produces our food and clothing? Are they paid properly for their work? Yes, it is better for people to have some work rather than none, but will we really pay more and own less so that others can live?

84 Three different words for our evil are used. Our offences are the ways in which we rebel or object to the ways of the LORD. Sins are the specific times we break His law or go against Him. "The interior word iniquities is used of the deviant state of the heart" (Motyer, 487).

Isaiah

God, revolt, oppression and lies are the many and terrible fruits of our condition (verse 13). That is why our lives and communities are the way they are: justice, goodness and truth are absent from our social life together (verse 14). In fact those who really do try to do what is right are persecuted (verse 15).

So, as the LORD looks not just at His own people but at the whole world He concludes that nobody is righteous, nobody is good. Nobody can save humanity... unless the LORD does it for Himself (verses 16-21). Christ the LORD is the only righteous person; the Holy One of Israel. He alone can put on righteousness and with great determination (verse 17), achieve salvation for His people. He will sort out the world, judging the wicked and gathering together all those who fear Him from all over the world (verses 18-20). He will come to Zion and save the people of Israel too who repent of their sins (verse 20).

Once again the Father speaks to Him (verse 21). The Father tells Christ that His Spirit will be on Him and His words will always be in His mouth so that He will be able to gather His family together forever and ever – verse 21.

Study 9 Bible Questions

Isaiah 57:11-21

1. Verse 11. What were the fears and worries that occupied the hearts and minds of the ancient Church in Isaiah's day? What are the fears and worries that have the same effect on the Church today?

2. Verse 11b. Why do we find it so hard to walk by faith and not by sight? If we do not see or hear the LORD God almost all the time, why do we so quickly stop trusting Him?

3. Verse 12. Why does the LORD point at "your righteousness and your works"?

4. Verse 13. Compare the refuge offered by the idols with the refuge offered by the LORD Jesus Christ.

5. Verse 14. Why does the LORD command this obstacle-free road to be built?

6. Verse 15. How can the Living God live both in the highest heaven and also in the lowliest heart? What does this tell us about the nature and glory of the Father, Son and Holy Spirit?

7. Verse 16-18. What do we learn here about the anger of the Living God? How does His anger compare to human anger?

8. Verses 19-21. In Jeremiah 6:14 the false prophets preach "peace, peace" when there is no peace. How does their false message compare to the preaching of the LORD Himself? Is it fair to say that the message of "peace, peace" must be preached to the Lord's people rather than to the wicked?

9. One of the great challenges that many are facing today is how to live in loving friendship with people who either ignore, reject or misunderstand the Way of Jesus. Many of our friends, families and neighbours follow belief systems that are committed to other gods or philosophies, and have a very different view of Jesus. What would Isaiah have thought of the idea that as long as people are sincere or open to love in whatever beliefs they have the LORD God might just welcome them into the new creation anyway?

Isaiah

Study 9 Further Questions

1. Thinking of Isaiah 57:1-2, what are the differences between the way Christians grieve and non-Christians grieve? How do we show this in our local Church life?

2. If Isaiah 56 challenged the ancient Church to include foreigners and eunuchs, then who are the people that we need to be challenged about? Who are the people that are missing from our local Church fellowship? If we look at the population profile of our local area, are there any obvious groups that are not represented? How would a Muslim feel if she wanted to visit one of our meetings? What about people who are not very good at reading? Do we have people with criminal records or people from 'difficult areas of town'? Are there as many men as women, young as old? Would a gay couple feel welcomed if they wanted to find out about Jesus? Is the Church leadership all of the same economic and social profile, and does this represent both the Church family and the local area?

Study 9 Daily Readings

Day 1	Isaiah 54:1-17
Day 2	Isaiah 55:1-13
Day 3	Isaiah 56:1-8
Day 4	Isaiah 56:9-57:13
Day 5	Isaiah 57:14-21
Day 6	Isaiah 58:1-14
Day 7	Isaiah 59:1-21

The daily Bible readings are an opportunity to not only read through all of the material in the book under study, but also to read parts of the Bible that relate to the themes and issues that we have been considering. We try to make sure that we receive light from the whole Bible as we think through the key issues each week.

The United Nations of Christ

Isaiah

Study 10 The Glory of the New Creation: Isaiah 60:1-66:24

KEY TRUTH
Christ the LORD is returning to renew the heavens and the earth as the everlasting home of righteousness

1. Arise, shine, for your light has come: 60:1-62:12

2. Oh that You would come down: 63:1-64:12

3. I will create new heavens and a new earth: 65:1-66:24

1. *Arise, shine, for your light has come* – 60:1-62:12

The Glory of Christ in Zion – (60:1-22)

The Redeemer comes to Zion – and when Jesus comes to His people it is the dawn of a new day. Arise, wake up, be resurrected, because the glory of Jesus is shining on you!

In chapter 59 we saw how the thick darkness of sin is lying over the whole world: no-one is righteous and our sins mount up, ruining our lives and destroying society. Yet, Christ the LORD rises like the sun and the darkness is driven away (60:1-2). All the different nations of the world will come to the light of Christ: His glory attracts the whole world (verse 3).

From all the Gentiles nations Zion's children come (verse 4). The glory and treasures of all the nations will come into Zion (see Revelation 21:22-27). The Church's great joy will come from seeing the glory of Jesus expand out across the whole world as more and more people join His kingdom (verse 5).

Notice who will be part of the global Church: Midianites and Egyptians (verse 6), but also the descendants of Ishamel will be Christians too (followers of Christ, whether looking forward to Him in the Old Testament or looking back to Him in the New Testament). The sons of Ishmael will be welcome to make offerings at the temple (verse 7). Even the islands and places as far away as Spain (Tarshish) will all come to honour Christ, the Holy One of Israel (verses 8-9).

The gates of Zion will be open and maintained by Gentile people from all over the world (verses 10-11). So much of this is picked up in Revelation 21 in the final description of the City of God.

Any people or nations who will not serve the Church and honour Christ will perish (verse 12). There is no future for those who will not humbly call on His name.

Zion will be known as Christ's city and the best of the earth will adorn her (60:13-17). This vision of the new creation and the City of God carries us higher and higher into wonder, love and praise. Christ will renew the world so comprehensively that there will be no more violence or destruction (verse 18), so the city will not need military walls. Instead her walls will simply be salvation and praise (verse 18b).

If we remember that the Light began to shine before any created light sources (Genesis 1:3) then we realise that the sun and moon are only weak creatures giving us a mere idea of that true uncreated Light of Christ. In that glorious resurrection future He will once again shine across the whole creation, filling everything with His light and life, driving out all sorrow, death and pain. Then it will be the opposite of chapter 59 because everyone will be righteous, yes, every single one (60:21). This means that there will never again be even the slightest danger of curses and exile driving us out of the land (verse 21). Even the very least of the righteous will have the blessings of Abraham (verse 22).

The Spirit-Filled Preacher – (61:1-11)

In Luke's biography of Jesus, chapter 4 verse 18-19, Jesus specifically states that Isaiah 61:1-2 was spoken about Him, and as soon as we read Isaiah's prophecy it is obvious that Isaiah was intending to point his original audience to the ministry of Jesus Christ. By definition Christ is always full of the Spirit, but the Spirit empowers Him for His mission of preaching good news to the poor, binding the broken-hearted, announcing freedom for captives and prisoners. Notice that He preaches the *year* of the LORD's favour and the *day* of His vengeance (verse 2) – His favour is so much more than His vengeance.

> "In his reading, the Lord Jesus stopped at the words *the Lord's favour* (2a) and did not proceed to *the day of vengeance*. Thus he expressed his own understanding of his mission at that point, not to condemn but to save the world (John 3:17). He was also aware, however, of a coming day when he would execute the judgment committed to him (John 5:22-29)" (Motyer, 500).

Jesus tells us that there is a longer time "a year" of the LORD's favour but there will finally be that day of vengeance.

Perhaps we are used to thinking fearfully or nervously about that day of vengeance, but in this last section of Isaiah it is clearly a day of great joy and victory for the Church. Zion has been persecuted for so long, suffering the schemes and abuse of the wicked. We have even grown weary of the sin in our own lives. We long for that day when everything will finally be put right and the whole creation will be set in everlasting order as the home of righteousness.

In one sense we may have grown so used to thinking of that final day from the perspective of the wicked that we have forgotten how to view it from the perspective of the righteous.

Isaiah tells us that the day of vengeance will be the day when those who mourn are finally comforted (2a). There will be no more death then and we will meet up with all the saints of every age in the presence of Jesus. Instead of the ashes of grief on our heads will be a crown of beauty and oil of joy. We may well feel despair right now in our exile and sorrow, but then we will be clothed with nothing but joy (verse 3). We will be like mighty oaks, solid and splendid, all to the praise of Christ.

All the ruins of this old world will be rebuilt and restored. All the nations of the world will come together to look after the heritage of Zion (verses 4-6). Everlasting joy and a rich inheritance will replace the shame and disgrace we knew in this passing age (verse 7).

Why? Because the day of vengeance will be when the LORD gets His way, making the world into the place that He always planned for it.

It was always going to be the family home of righteousness, the home of the Divine Bridegroom and His Bride forever and ever. He will fill the world with justice and drive out all the hated wrongdoing (verse 8). His everlasting marriage covenant will be established (verses 8-11), and clothed in righteous robes the Bridegroom and Bride, the Great High Priest of all creation and His Beloved, will fulfil the destiny of the whole creation.

The Bridegroom and His Bride (62:1-12)

That vision of the marriage of Christ and the Church is the driving force behind the renewal of the heavens and the earth. Christ's day of resurrection and judgment is all for the sake of Zion, for His Bride. He is determined to make her righteousness shine out like the dawn (verse 1). He wants the Church to be the centre of wonder and attention as her own reflected glory is displayed (verse 2). She will seem so different than she was in this old age that she will have a new name given to her by Christ, a new name that reflects her true nature. The Church is nothing less than Christ's crown and sceptre (verse 3).

Her new name reflects the fact that she was once called Deserted and Desolate, but then will be known as *Hephzibah* living in Beulah – Christ delights in being married to her! Yes, Christ will be just as excited about His marriage as a young man on his wedding day. The Living God will rejoice over His Church (verse 5).

We are now called to constantly pray, constantly call on the LORD to make this happen. Jesus Himself told us to daily pray that His Kingdom would come (62:6-7).

The LORD has promised this future and we can keep on reminding Him of His promise, day and night (verses 8-9). These promises of blessing take us right back to the blessings of Deuteronomy 28:1-14, with the opposite of the curses.

The whole earth must be made ready for this future (verses 10-12). To the ends of the earth all people are summoned to see Christ the LORD coming with His reward to Zion, His Bride. The whole world will seek after Zion when they hear of this (verse 12b).

Isaiah

2. *Oh that You would come down* – 63:1-64:12

The Day of Vengeance (63:1-6)

Yet, the preparation for the new creation as the home of righteousness has to be the day of vengeance and judgment. The world cannot be that place of righteousness, joy and peace until it has been cleansed from all the wickedness and evil. There can be no place for even the slightest trace of evil if the marriage home is to be safe forever and ever.

So, Christ will first come, filled with the furious and holy anger of the Living God on that day of vengeance. Isaiah sees Christ coming from the land of Edom in robes splattered with blood. This time it is Edom that represents the wicked of the world, just as it was Moab in chapter 25. Christ is gloriously robed for His wedding day, but first He must prepare the family home. Christ is righteous in His judgment (verse 1) and the greatness of His strength means that nothing will stop Him bringing this salvation to His world. Nobody helps Him (verse 3) as He destroys the wicked from all over the world. He does this work alone in His anger.

Notice again in verse 4 how the day of vengeance is the time for Him to redeem. The day of God's wrath is the great and glorious day when goodness, truth, justice and joy are given free reign forever and ever: the day when greed, lies, selfishness and sin are judged and destroyed forever and ever.

On that day the nations will be forced to drink that cup of God's wrath (51:17-23), yet they cannot survive such a drink and their blood will be poured on the ground (verse 6).

As Isaiah's declarations of the glory of the new creation get ever brighter, so his clarity about the day of vengeance gets ever sharper.

The Shepherd of the Flock – (63:7-19)

With that stark vision of Christ on the day of vengeance so vividly before us, Isaiah now tells us of the great kindness and compassion of the Father (63:7).[85]

---

85 See verse 16 when this LORD is specifically addressed as the Father.

He wanted to save His children and make them true to Him (verse 8), so He sent the Divine Angel, Christ (verse 9) together with His Holy Spirit to save them. The whole Trinity is involved in this work of salvation for the Church – Father, Son and Spirit. Isaiah reviews how this happened during the Exodus when the Angel of the LORD, who commissioned Moses at the burning bush (Exodus 3:1-6), came to rescue His people. He redeemed them out of Egypt, carrying them through the desert (see Judges 2:1). The Holy Spirit was with them and they actually rebelled against Him with constant grumbling and unbelief (verse 10).

Yet, says Isaiah, His people are turning to Him again. They want the Father to send again the Angel of the LORD, the Good Shepherd of the Flock and they want Him to pour out His Spirit upon them (verse 11). Just as the Spirit and Christ were with them in the Exodus, so that could happen again (verse 13-14). Verse 15 is the heart of the prayer: appealing to the nature and the character of our heavenly Father. Verse 16 sounds strange but "the sense of the verse is that where even the greatest and most honoured members of the family can offer no help, the Fatherhood of the Lord and his Redeemer-kinship is still available and avails" (Motyer, 516).

Our only hope is that the Father will send His Spirit to change our hearts (verse 17). We know that we cannot change ourselves.

Isaiah imagines how the Church will pray when in exile in Babylon – verses 18-19. Jerusalem has been desecrated by her enemies, but for the sake of those ancient promises the LORD should restore His people.

Oh that you would come down! (64:1-12)

There is nothing that we can do to redeem or restore. Political alliances are of no use and human religion is powerless. Oh that the Living God would come down and show His glory and power here! Oh that He would come for His day of vengeance and redemption! (Verse 1)

When Christ comes in all His uncreated glory, then His enemies will know Him and the nations will quake (verse 2). Again, remembering the Exodus when the LORD came down to Sinai and made the mountains tremble, it would be marvellous for the LORD to act in that way again (verse 3).

Isaiah

The other 'gods' are all talk and myth. These 'gods' might sound impressive on paper or in philosophy, but where are they in history? What have any of them actually done that we can see in the concrete real world? (Verse 4). The LORD God really does act for those who wait for Him (verse 5).

Yet if we don't wait on the LORD and instead we are lost in our sin, provoking His anger, then what will happen? Even our very best and most righteous acts are nothing but used menstrual cloths or like shrivelled up leaves (verse 6). Our sins have hidden the LORD's face from us and our sins leave us wasting and withering away (verses 6-7).

Yet, the Father made us and we are the work of His hands. In our sin we sometimes think we can make or heal or improve or restore ourselves, but in truth we are simply clay in the Father's hands (verse 8). Our only hope is that the anger of God is turned away from us and that our sins would be forgotten (verse 9). Instead of hiding His face from us, we need Him to actually look upon us (verse 9).

Isaiah reminds the Father of the terrible state of Jerusalem and the temple (verses 11-12). Surely He would not forget His people in exile and would restore them for His own sake.

3. *I will create new heavens and a new earth* – 65:1-66:24

All day long... (65:1-16)

The glorious good news is that the LORD God does not wait for people to find Him or call on Him. He reveals Himself to those who do not ask or seek (65:1). Back in chapter 6 it was Isaiah who called out "here I am" in response to the LORD's call, but here it is the LORD Himself crying out "here I am!" even when sinful humanity is not calling for Him at all (verse 1b).

Given that nobody in the world is righteous and nobody could survive His day of judgment, the LORD God spends all day stretching out His hands and calling to people who are stubborn and do all they can to provoke Him.

This is such a remarkable part of the Bible, where the patient commitment of the LORD to winning us sinners is made so very clear.

He lists all the ways people provoke Him, doing the very things that most anger and offend Him:

- Pagan worship – verse 3
- Worship of the dead – verse 4
- Eating the very foods that the Law described as unclean – verse 4
- YET, pretending to be so religious – verse 5.

According to the Law, according to what is written, the LORD should destroy them for these sins, paying them back in full – verses 6-7. However, that is not how the LORD will treat His people. He will restore those who trust Him and bring them to their land, the mountains of the LORD (verses 8-10). But, those who insist on carrying on with their pagan religion (verse 11) will be judged and destroyed (verse 12). Even when the LORD came looking for them and calling for Him, still they would not listen.

So, there will be a clear contrast between those who respond to His calling and those who carry on with their sinful rebellion – verses 13-14.

The LORD's people will eat, drink, rejoice and sing; whereas those that still will not listen to Him will go hungry and thirsty; they will face shame and anguish – verses 13-14. It is death for the wicked, but life and blessing in the land for His people.

New heavens and the new earth (65:17-25)

In fact, the past troubles will be so completely forgotten (verse 16) because the entire cosmos is going to be re-ordered and redeemed. The heavens and the earth will be so thoroughly filled with Christ's glory and joy that they will be a new creation! (65:17).

This old passing order will be forgotten with all its sin, shame and pain. Rather, our hearts and minds will be completely filled with that new creation. Zion, the City of God – the heavenly Jerusalem – will be all that it was supposed to be: a place of delight and joy so wonderful that even Christ Himself will rejoice over it. All sorrow and weeping will be gone forever (65:19).

Death will be gone. Never again will children die in infancy and we will never again have to deal with the pain and bitterness of dying in the

Isaiah

middle of our years (verse 20). This verse "does not imply that death will still be present (contradicting 25:7-8) but rather affirms that over the whole of life, as we should now say from infancy to old age, the power of death will be destroyed" (Motyer, 530).

Deuteronomy 28 warned that the curses of sin will mean that the LORD's people will build houses and others will live in them and others will eat the crops they have worked to grow. So, by contrast, in our resurrection future we will have houses and vineyards that belong to us, that we will be able to enjoy for ourselves (verse 21-23). All the curses of sin will be gone forever. The LORD will be so near and so attentive to His pure and righteous people that He will respond before they have finished asking (verse 24).

Once again we are reminded how this redemption is not just for human beings, but for the whole creation including the animals (65:25).

The LORD is coming (66:1-24)

Isaiah has given us such a clear and glorious vision of reality. The whole world is filled with the glory of Christ – the Divine King; the Holy One of Israel; the Bridegroom; the Angel of the LORD. He is high above all the nations of the world and nothing in all creation can compare to Him, and yet He would be born of a virgin woman becoming a lowly human being. Filled with the Spirit Christ would preach His good news and live the life that none of us could ever live. He would be rejected and killed by us, yet even this was the will of the Father so that Jesus would die as a sacrificial lamb with all our sins laid upon Him. Yet, even when the LORD suffered His own furious wrath against sin on our behalf, He was resurrected and ascended to the highest heaven to intercede for His people. Though the Church lives in exile in Babylon – whether literally in the city of Babylon as the later readers of Isaiah were, or symbolically as the Church in every age has been – we are sustained by the glorious hope that is set before us. A day of vengeance and resurrection is coming, the wedding day of Christ and the Church. On that day He will first judge the world, pouring out His divine wrath on all the wicked to take them away for ever. Yet, this judgment is done to prepare the heavens and the earth to be redeemed and reordered as the everlasting home of righteousness.

In this final chapter all of these themes are gathered together.

The people of Isaiah's day needed to know that the temple that was in Jerusalem was not the most important thing. It would be destroyed when they were taken into exile and would be finished once for all after Christ had completed His work. So, the LORD declares that if heaven is His throne and earth is His footstool what kind of temple could any of us possibly build for Him? (Verse 1).

Rather, He will dwell with anyone who is contrite and broken (57:15). That is the key to true worship. Merely slaughtering bulls and lambs was actually sinful and offensive when it was offered as an alternative to that true worship of the heart. Those that do not listen or respond to the LORD will face a future with the very things they most dread (verses 3-4).

Verses 5-6 show that within Israel (considered as those who were simply part of that ancient earthly nation) there was a very deep division between those who genuinely trembled at the Word of God and those who mocked at such things. The mockers hated those people who loved the LORD and would say "you are always going on about the glory of Christ! The only thing that seems to make you joyful is the LORD's glory. Let's see this glory so that you can finally have your strange joy!" – verse 5. The LORD promises that even though those people are perhaps genetically children of Abraham, yet there is nothing for them but death and destruction (verse 6).

The LORD God describes Zion as producing many children – an idea that He has set before us many times throughout the book. She will give birth to all her children with no labour pains. In fact she will give birth in a moment, a whole nation in a day – verses 7-13.[86]

---

[86] "...this was a figure of the setting up of the Christian Church in the world, and the replenishing of that family with children which was to be named from Jesus Christ. When the Spirit was poured out, and the gospel went forth from Zion, multitudes were converted in a little time and with little pains compared with the vast product. The apostles, even before they travailed, brought forth, and the children born to Christ were so numerous, and so suddenly and easily produced, that they were rather like the dew from the morning's womb than like the son from the mother's womb, Ps. cx. 3. The success of the gospel was astonishing; that light, like the morning, strangely diffused itself till it took hold even of the ends of the earth. Cities and nations were born at once to Christ. The same day that the Spirit was poured out there were 3000 souls added to the Church. And, when this glorious work was once begun, it was carried on wonderfully, beyond what could be imagined, so mightily grew the word of God and prevailed" (Matthew Henry).

Isaiah

The LORD is coming. To the Church that thought makes our hearts rejoice, but His enemies must face His fury (verses 14-15).

The LORD is coming with fire to purge the world. He comes with His furious anger and with flames of fire to destroy all the wicked with their pagan worship and disregard for the Law of the LORD – verses 15-17.

Yet, Christ's glory must first be displayed to all the nations (verses 18-21). People of every nation and language (verse 18) will see His glory – from as far away as Tarshish in Spain or Libya in North Africa or Greece or even more distant islands like Great Britain or Australia or Indonesia or Japan (verse 19). Verse 20 states quite plainly that the Church will find brothers in all the nations of the world, just as Psalm 87 said. Yes, those Gentiles will be so completely joined to Israel/the Church that they could even serve as Aaronic or Levitical priests at the temple.

The new heavens and the new earth are our true home: a home that will last forever and ever (verse 22). This old form of the universe is decaying and wearing out, but that resurrection age will never wear out. All humanity will be part of that new creation, yet those who refused and rebelled will have no future there at all. Whereas the righteous have immortal bodies, the bodies of the wicked having been destroyed by the LORD with His furious anger will simply be piled up and left to be eaten by the worms: worms who will never be satisfied. However arrogant the wicked might be in this passing age, when Christ comes they will have no honour at all. In fact, all that will be left of them will be "loathsome to all mankind" (66:24).

In the end, when all has been put right, the vain glory and shame of evil and darkness will finally be thrown away into the rubbish tip of the outer darkness forever and ever. Yet, the glory of the LORD Jesus Christ will finally be unrivalled, filling the whole creation. Christ and His Bride will enjoy that new creation forever and ever, revelling in that eternal life of God free from the dangers of sin and evil once and for all.

Study 10 Bible Questions

Isaiah 62:1-63:6

1. Verse 1. This is one of the most emotionally intense parts of the whole Bible as we see the LORD God as the loving husband of His new bride (62:4-5) but also as He comes in saving judgment against the world (63:1-6). So, what is the great passion that motivates the great redemption plans of the Living God?

2. Verses 2-3. With all the kings of the earth looking to the Great King, where does His Church, fit in this picture?

3. Verses 4-5. Verse 2 mentioned a new name and now we learn what it is: Hephzibah (my delight is in her); and the name of the land is Beulah (married). Thinking about the beginning and end of the Bible, how do these verses take us to the very heart of the meaning of the universe itself?

4. Verses 6-7. How do these verses connect to the Lord's Prayer – "may your kingdom come and your will be done on earth as in heaven"?

5. Verses 8-9. Looking ahead to that time when the City of God is established in the new creation, compare these verses with the description of the resurrection future in 65:21-22.

6. Verses 10-12. Why would a message about "the Daughter of Zion" be proclaimed to the ends of the earth?

7. Verses 1-3. Throughout the book of Isaiah we have often seen how the Holy One of Israel is all alone in His righteousness and opposition to evil, but here that fact strikes home with a vivid intensity. Why has the reality of the winepress of God's wrath been seen as such good news by millions of people down through history?

> Mine eyes have seen the glory of the coming of the Lord:
> He is trampling out the vintage where the grapes of wrath are stored;
> He hath loosed the fateful lightning of His terrible swift sword:
> His truth is marching on.

Isaiah

    Glory, glory, hallelujah!
    Glory, glory, hallelujah!
    Glory, glory, hallelujah!
    His truth is marching on.

8. Verses 4-6. What is the great motivation of Christ the LORD in His lonely work?

Study 10 Further Questions

1. Why does Isaiah end his book with such a grim scene? What is the effect of this on his readers?

2. Isaiah 66:3 is used by certain kinds of vegetarians to say that killing an animal is equivalent to murder. Is this the point that Isaiah is making?

3. What will the economic system of the new creation be like, given Isaiah 65:21-23? Will everything simply be shared together? If the skills and talents we have right now are brought to their perfection and maturity in that resurrection future, then will some people work as artists, scientists, musicians, engineers, cooks, authors, athletes, film-makers and administrators? Will all of us be self-sufficient with our own farms, or will food production also be according to ability and desire?

Study 10 Daily Readings

Day 1	Isaiah 60:1-22
Day 2	Isaiah 61:1-11
Day 3	Isaiah 62:1-12
Day 4	Isaiah 63:1-19
Day 5	Isaiah 64:1-12
Day 6	Isaiah 65:1-25
Day 7	Isaiah 66:1-24

The daily Bible readings are an opportunity to not only read through all of the material in the book under study, but also to read parts of the Bible that relate to the themes and issues that we have been considering. We try to make sure that we receive light from the whole Bible as we think through the key issues each week.

Isaiah

Suggested Answers to the Bible Study Questions

Study 1   Bible Answers

Isaiah 2:1-22

1. Verse 2. Isaiah looks into the future, beyond the Jerusalem of his day, at the new creation and the Mountain of the LORD (see Hebrews 12:22). Given the judgment on Jerusalem described in chapter 1, what was the purpose of this prophecy of 'the last days'?

The great 19th century preacher C. H. Spurgeon said that for every look at self we need to take five looks at the LORD Jesus Christ. When we are confronted with our sinfulness or the corruption of the "city of man" then we need to fix our hearts and minds on the purity, holiness, beauty and glory of Christ's "city of God" that is in the highest heavens; the city that will come down from heaven to the earth on that final day – see Revelation 21:1-2. It is vital to see how everything will end up in "the last days" so that we see everything around us right now with the proper perspective.

2. Verses 2b-3. Think about the fears of the people of Jerusalem, in terms of the armies and empires threatening them. How does the LORD's view of the world differ from theirs? How do these words still speak to us today?

It is so easy to see only danger and darkness where the LORD sees opportunities and need. The great problem that Isaiah was confronting was the way the people were full of fear about the surrounding nations, unable to trust the LORD about the future and therefore unable to witness to these nations about the true Rock of safety and security. Instead of seeing the nations as threats, the LORD shows them how the Church would cover all the nations. People from even the most pagan nations will be setting their hearts and minds on that glorious City of God. The Gentiles were not to be feared but won, grafted onto the vine of Israel.

3. Verse 4-5. Is this vision of a war-free world simply about our new creation future? What does it mean to live now with that hope in front of us? How does verse 5 relate to this?

We can easily see how Christ the LORD will come to get rid of all violence and division when He comes to judge the world. In that new creation world there can be no more war. However, these words are to shape us

Isaiah

even now. If we have this hope in us now then we purify ourselves right now from such evil (see 2 Peter 3:11 and 1 John 3:3). People should be able to see a preview of the society of the new creation whenever they come to Church.

4. Verses 6-8. The contrast with the state of Jerusalem in Isaiah's day is strong. List all the ways that the ancient Church had turned away from that new creation hope that Christ would bring.

- Forsaken the fellowship of the saints ("abandoned your people");
- Fallen into pagan superstitions;
- Followed "fortune telling" practices, whether palm reading, horoscopes or whatever ways the Philistines followed;
- Fellowshipped with pagan people, clasping hands as if there was nothing to divide us;[87]
- Stored up treasure on earth, "no end to their treasures";
- Trusted in their own strength or power for security, "no end to their chariots";
- Worshipping the things they have made, looking to mere physical creations to give them the peace and fulfilment that only the LORD Jesus can give.

5. Verse 9-12. It is as if Isaiah prays that the LORD will set everything right in verse 9. What is the final answer to this prayer?

Over and over again throughout the book of Isaiah we are confronted with the sheer scale and depth of the sin, selfishness and shame of the human condition. Each time we are also shown how all this has to be thrown away on that final day of judgment. There can be absolutely no future for such worthless things. We dare not cling onto these things for a moment longer and we need to clearly see that they will drag us down to Hell. "The LORD Almighty has a day in store" is the great truth that we will face time after time in Isaiah. The problems of the world will all be resolved on that final day, even though we may taste something of that while we wait.

---

87 It is important to note the difference between, on the one hand, loving and serving the people around us who are not yet Christians and on the other hand giving the impression that we share the same beliefs or that our beliefs do not make any difference. Jesus Himself shared table fellowship with the most notorious sinners (including people like you and me), but He also shone His light in the darkness, calling on these beloved people to turn away from unbelief and follow Him

6. Verses 13-18. How do all these images help us to understand what will happen on the Day of the LORD?

In all these images we see the things that are tall and strong brought down low. Isaiah gets into the hearts and minds of his audience looking at all the things that seem to make a statement about what is strong and enduring; what represents power and stability: strong cedars and oaks; towering mountains; lofty towers; fortified walls; tall ships. All these things will be brought down low and shaken. Everything that can be shaken will be shaken down on that day the LORD Almighty has in store (Hebrews 12:27).

7. Verses 19-21. When the skies are filled with the glory of Christ the LORD, the arrogant world will try to flee underground. How does Isaiah show the revolution of that day?

In the previous verses we were shown all the things that stand tall, but now we are burrowing under the ground in caves. Now we are shown the bats and rats in the potholes of the ground as people try to go down as low as possible to escape from the dread and splendid majesty of the LORD. When He arrives all that seemed so tall and strong is shown up and rather than trying to stand tall, arrogant humanity will throw away the things they thought would protect them and cower away in the dark depths.

8. Verse 22. This summary verse gives us one of the deep truths of the whole Bible. How do we feel this challenge in our own lives today?

Isaiah

Study 2 Bible Answers

Isaiah 11:1-11

1. Verse 1. What is the meaning of the reference to Jesse? (see 1 Samuel 16:1). Why is it important to know that a shoot is coming from the stump of Jesse? (see 2 Samuel 7:12-13)

The promise of the Messiah-King was made in such a strong way to David: after David had died he would have a descendant who would establish God's kingdom forever and ever. At his best David gave the ancient Church a glimpse of what it would be like when Jesus was born among them. It might have looked as if the whole of Israel and Judah were going to be wiped out, but from the stump of Jesse there would be One, the Holy One of Israel, who would maintain His people.

2. Verse 2. What does the word 'Messiah' (Hebrew) or 'Christ' (Greek) actually mean? Why is that relevant to the prophecy of verse 2?

'Messiah' or 'Christ' simply means 'the one anointed with oil' or when speaking of Jesus Himself 'The One anointed with the Spirit'. The old priests, kings and prophets all had to be anointed with oil when they began their work to show that they needed the Holy Spirit to do all their work. To speak of this holistic and comprehensive work of the Spirit in the Son of David was a very powerful way of holding up the Divine Messiah before the eyes of the ancient Church.

3. We sometimes say that everything that God does is "from the Father, through the Son and in the power of the Spirit". How does this help us to appreciate verse 2?

Throughout Isaiah we see several examples of the Messiah sent from the LORD in the power of the Spirit. In one sense we could say that it is the LORD sent from the LORD with the LORD, but it is usually more helpful to identify whether we are speaking of Christ, His Father or the Spirit. Notice how everything that Christ does and all His most basic qualities are filled with the Spirit. Even His "fear of the LORD" – the way that He relates to His Father – is Spirit-filled. It is glorious to see how the One Living God is so tightly bound together, all wrapped up in the fellowship of the Father, Son and Holy Spirit. This One God can only be thought of when we think of all Three together.

4. Verse 3-4a. What is wrong with judging by what we see or hear? How do His judgments for the poor and needy show this?

Our judgments are all too often very superficial, only based on how things appear to us. Stories about criminal investigations that cut through appearances to get to the truth are ever popular because we realise how surface judgments are rarely adequate. The poor and the needy are used to 'justice' only going for those with power and privilege, but the LORD Jesus Christ will not be swayed by the status or wealth of anybody no matter how much (or how little) they have.

5. Verse 4b. Why is important to know that Christ the LORD will ultimately strike the earth in judgment even though He first comes as the Suffering Servant?

The reason we can always turn the other cheek and "for your sake face death all day long; we are considered as sheep to be slaughtered" (Romans 8:36; Psalm 44:22) is because we know that there will be a Day of Justice when everything will be put right. We do not need to take vengeance on anybody because we know that it is the job of the LORD God alone to do that most difficult job. Jesus first offers grace and forgiveness for everybody, even for those who have done the worst of all crimes, but if they will not allow Him to face the judgment for them then there will be a day when they must face that vengeance alone.

6. Verses 6-8. For the animals to behave like this there would need to be far more than a superficial change to the world. Why does Isaiah pick these combinations of animals? How does this holistic vision of the animal world remind us of Eden at the beginning?

These combinations of animals seem the most impossible of all! We all react to these ideas: predators becoming vegetarians; lions grazing like cattle! He might also have spoken of sharks snacking on seaweed! These images were no less shocking to the people of his day than the modern world. The point is that the new world order is so much more than "re-arranging the furniture". A whole new order of ecology and physics, a fundamentally new order of existence itself, is held up before us. Genesis 1:29-31 seems to suggest that the original plan was for all the animals to be vegetarian.

Isaiah

7. Verse 9. What is the fundamental explanation for the radically new biological order of the world?

The real change in the world goes deeper than biology or physics. These material 'laws' are only ever superficial expressions of much deeper realities: the relationship of the Living God to His creation. When the whole creation is properly united to the Living God and the knowledge of Him fills all things, then this new order of the heavens and earth will follow on.

8. Verses 10-11. What is the centre-piece and climax of the new creation? What is the goal of Christ's redemption?

Just as the creation of Genesis 1 came to its climax and goal with the creation of humanity, so the new creation finds its centre in the Church of the Living God. All the nations of the world are drawn back together around the LORD Jesus Christ. He personally stands as the rallying point for the people from all the pagan nations around Israel.

Study 3 Bible Answers

Isaiah 17:1-14

1. Verses 1-3. Damascus was the capital of the kingdom of Aram, yet the LORD announced a judgment of destruction against it such that flocks of sheep will be free to graze right where the mighty city once stood. Why did the Arameans (and us still today) need to know that no matter how impressive our cities might be, they have no future?

We are surrounded with buildings, culture and life that seems to be here forever. We tend to see the cities, empires and even the people who are so powerful today as if they were always going to be just as they are right now. Yet, how many of the great cities of the ancient world have left even ruins for us to see? Are any of the mighty empires of Isaiah's day still around? The constant need is for us to set our hearts and minds on that unseen world of Jesus Christ, the coming world of the future because everything we can see will pass away.

2. Verse 4. Why does Isaiah make us think of Jacob as a large man who has wasted away with age and illness?

The constant theme of the chapter is the fleeting nature of human glory and strength. What today seems so strong will fade away and disappear before long. Only the Living God lasts forever. So, we might imagine a big man, full of life and filling his mouth with good things, but how quickly he can become a shadow of himself through age or illness. That small old man was once a force to be reckoned with. If we forget this we will be deceived ny passing human glory.

3. Verses 5-6. Another image shows us the corn field and the olive orchard after the harvest has finished. What is the power of this image? Is there any hope at all?

A field of corn ready for harvest seems so full of vitality and life, yet that same field the day after the harvest seems so lifeless and feeble. The few remaining stalks only highlight how empty it is. The few remaining olives on the bare branches only remind us that everyhing is gone. Today human glory seems so impressive but tomorrow it is all gone.

Isaiah

4. Verse 7-8. What is the purpose behind this cutting down of human pride? Who is our Maker and who is 'the Holy One of Israel'? Is the fundamental character of an idol that it is "the work of (our) hands"?

The LORD, throughout the book of Isaiah, brings this kind of judgment on the different nations so that they will abandon their own vain glory and flee to the eternal glory of Christ the LORD. God the Father is our Maker and Jesus Christ is the Holy One of Israel, as Peter reminded the crowd in Acts 3:14. Idols may change from one culture to the next, but in one sense they are always the same: the work of our hands. Whether it is an ancient statue of Baal or an entertainment system in the corner of our room, if we expect mere human creations to give us peace or fulfilment we are worshipping an idol.

5. Verse 9. Imagine the city or town where we live being deserted and overgrown with weeds. How does this change our perspective on the life or 'glory' of that town or city?

We can so easily be caught up into the values and 'treasures' of this passing "City of Man". If we lose sight of Christ then we might fear what others think of us and chase after things that we cannot hold onto.

6. Verses 10-11. The apostle Paul reminds us that the Rock of Israel was Christ Himself (1 Corinthians 10:4). What happened when those ancient people forgot Him?

When they were no longer building on the eternal Rock of Christ the LORD then they had no future. Yes, they could make plans and act as if they had a future, but in truth it was all in vain. The day of disease and death came to them, as to all flesh, and they had no substance. When we forget Christ the Rock then we too will be forgotten.

7. Verses 12-13. How does Isaiah present the rising arrogance and pride of the nations? What is the response of the Rock to this raging sea?

The pride of the nations is like a raging sea whose waves rise up and threaten to sweep everything away. Human pride makes us think of ourselves as far more powerful and longer lasting than we really are. Just as the LORD God was able to make the Red Sea retreat before Him,

so all the rage of the nations disappears as soon as He rebukes them. See Psalm 2 for more of this.

8. Verse 14. Sudden disaster can take any or all of us away. What is Isaiah's message as we face such an uncertain future?

There is a Rock even in the worst storm of life. In chapter 40 of Isaiah we are bluntly told that all flesh is grass: here today and gone tomorrow. Yet, the Word of God endures forever and if we trust Him then He shares that eternal life with us. Yes, we are pilgrims here and (as Hezekiah discovers in chapter 38) we may die when we least expect it, but Christ will never forsake us and He will bring us to Himself and on into His everlasting new creation future.

Isaiah

Study 4 Bible Answers

Isaiah 26:1-13

1. Verse 1. In chapter 24 Isaiah confronted us with the destruction of the whole earth under the LORD's judgment. Even the powers in the heavens will be judged (24:21). The cities of this age will all crumble away (25:2). However, what enduring hope does the Church have in every age?

There is a city with foundations whose Builder and Maker is God – Hebrews 11:10. Abraham himself had his heart and mind fixed on that City of God in the highest heavens, so we too need to always remember our home in Zion. Yes, we look forward to that final day when the City of God will come down to the earth, but even now that "strong city" is our true home in the heavens.

2. Verse 2. What is the entry requirement to enter into this strong and eternal city of God?

There is no way of getting into that Heavenly Jerusalem through human religion or personal 'righteousness' or self-improvement. Only those that "keep faith" may enter; those that trust the LORD Jesus Christ.

3. Verse 3. How can we have peace even when everything in our lives seems to be falling apart?

These people faced war and exile in their own lives. It is quite possible that they would lose their homes; their freedom; even their lives. Yet, like Daniel, Esther and Ezekiel, even in a distant pagan nation, with their names stripped from them and all the supports to their faith torn down, yet the LORD would still be with them giving them His own peace, a peace beyond understanding that the world cannot give. It is incredible how He draws especially near to us when we are broken-hearted, when it seems that peace is furthest from us.

4. Verse 4. How does Isaiah encourage us to trust in Christ the eternal Rock?

If everything in life seems to be falling apart and if chaos and death seem to be overwhelming us, then we need to know that Christ is the Eternal Rock. Jesus Christ is the same yesterday and today and forever. That was as true for Isaiah's day as it is for us. He is always the Eternal Rock: we can build upon Him and never be destroyed by even the worst storms of life. He will never leave us nor forsake us.

5. Verses 5-6. What is the alternative to trusting Him? What is the outcome of that?

If we do not trust Christ the LORD then we always end up trusting ourselves, whether trusting in our own abilities or the traditions, religion or philosophy that we think can save us. Instead of humbly trusting the LORD Himself, we lift ourselves up before Him. Not only will this attract His own judgment of us, but arrogant people tend to be brought down to earth by the people around them.

6. Verses 7-8. We might worry that the road ahead of us is completely broken and full of holes, but how can we walk on a level and smooth road through life? What must capture our hearts even when fears and pain surround us?

This again all comes down to trusting the LORD Jesus Christ, the Upright One. Jesus said "do not worry about tomorrow, for tomorrow will worry about itself. Each day has enough trouble of its own" (Matthew 6:34). We can only do this if we really do trust our heavenly Father to guide our steps through life. Yet, we must also take responsibility by making His Name and renown "the desire of our hearts". If our hearts are filled with love for comfort, treasure, ease and relationships then we will wander off the smooth path that He sets for us.

7. Verses 9-11. Describe the difference between the righteous and the wicked. Can we say they have different hearts and different eyes?

The righteous have fixed their hearts and minds on the Living God. He is their first thought in the morning and their meditation throughout the night. The righteous regard the majesty of the LORD, seeing all the things that He does and keeping the fear of Him always fresh in their hearts. However, the wicked are filled with their own worries throughout the night and think of themselves in the morning. The wicked do not learn the lessons that the LORD is trying to teach them. When sufferings under God's judgment come, they learn nothing from them. Even when the blessings and favour of the LORD are on the wicked, they assume it is just their right and learn nothing from that either. Instead of seeing the zeal of the LORD for His people (and therefore run to join these people), they go blindly on until they fall into the fire of destruction. The heart and eyes of the righteous are on the Living God, but the hearts and eyes of the wicked do not notice what is really going on.

8. Verse 12. How are we to think of the fruit we produce in life?

Everything that we do that has any value at all in our lives, even the desire to do what is good, is all from the work of the Father, Son and Holy Spirit – see Philippians 2:13.

9. Verse 13. How are we to cope with the forces and empires that try to control us? What can we do if even the government opposes us? How can we support our brothers and sisters who are in constant danger from oppressive regimes?

Many Christians live under regimes that not only do not acknowledge the LORD Jesus Christ but actually try to oppose Him and oppress His people. The Bible constantly teaches us that we must not fear them because we are so filled with a proper love and fear for the Living God. Consider the Hebrew midwives in Exodus 1:15-21 who feared the LORD rather than Pharaoh. We must always be faithful to our true LORD no matter what these little 'lords' tell us to do. It is vital that we support the Christian family around the world through prayer and by writing letters both to them and to the regimes that persecute them.

Study 5   Bible Answers

Isaiah 33:1-17

1. Verses 1, 3-4. With the Assyrian armies banging on the gates of the city and hard times ahead, Isaiah looks beyond the current troubles to the final destiny of all oppressors and wicked people. Why is it so important to always keep that final day of justice in mind?

This whole study makes us look at the unseen reality of Christ that lasts forever rather than the very visible troubles, fears and temptations that surround us. The Bible speaks so much about the way everything will be on the final Day of Justice so that we can keep that true prespective in the constant confusion of life in this passing age.

2. Verse 2. In the hardest times, the "time of distress" how can we find the strength to face each day?

The way we begin each day is essential. All our sinful desires and selfish thoughts will flood into our minds and control our day unless we begin the day with Christ Jesus Himself as the love of our hearts. Whether we initially feel much affection or not, we take control of our hearts and set Christ before us as the One we long for; our Strength and our salvation in time of distress.

3. Verse 5. It is all too easy to keep our eyes fixed on the troubles all around us – like Peter who focussed on the waves in Matthew 14:30. What is the remedy for this?

Jesus taught us to begin all our prayers with "Our Father in heaven…". The throneroom of heaven, the heavenly Zion, must always hold our vision: the Father with Jesus at His right hand. As soon as we allow our attention and worries to feed on the time of distress that we are facing, then we will sink.

4. Verse 6. Looking up to the King in Zion above, we are also aware of the foundation beneath our feet and the rich store of resources to get us through the time of distress. How do we unlock this rich store?

The fear of the LORD is the key to this treasure. In the time of distress – whether in our nations or in the troubles of our own life – fear is the great

Isaiah

powerful enemy. If we are driven by our fear of other people or our fear of death, then we will never be able to act wisely or keep a peaceful heart. The rich store of salvation, wisdom and knowledge is unlocked when we fear the LORD more than anything else. If we fear Him we have nothing else to fear: then we can think clearly and act with justice, integrity and love, keeping our hearts and minds fixed on Him.

5. Verses 7-9. Isaiah describes the land of Judah and the city of Jerusalem in the coming time of distress. List the different aspects that strike so deep. Imagine facing these troubles in our own cities or nation.

The bravest men, who are the hope of any nation in a time of war, are wandering around crying in the streets. The ambassadors who were sent to negotiate a peace treaty are weeping bitterly in their failure. The people are all gone: run away, exiled and killed. The streets are all empty and nobody dares to move freely about. The normal business agreeements that make civilisation possible are broken. There is no respect for authority. Even the land itself seems to waste away. With no one to work the land it quickly returns to wilderness. If we have experienced any serious civil disorder, we can see how accurate and frightening this description is.

6. Verses 10-12. How does the LORD exalt Himself in these verses? Is this good news or bad news, in the light of verses 7-9?

This is bad news for sin, wickedness and selfishness: they have no future and their own actions contribute to their own destruction. Yet, the wonderful good news is that history is not a meaningless chaos of good and evil endlessly fighting it out. No! The LORD God will arise and put everything right, exalting Himself when He gets rid of all the corrupting rubbish of this dark age.

7. Verses 13-15. Think back to the words in Isaiah 29:13 with their superficial understanding and empty devotion. Describe the contrast with 33:13-14.

When the sinners and godless are confronted by the concrete power and actions of the Living God, then all the illusions are dispelled. In our comfortable sin we imagine that everything is well, that we need not be

afraid of God, that He has only love and indulgence for us. When we see that the Living God is a consuming fire and that even the best of us can never dwell with His everlasting fire, then a true fear of the LORD may begin.

8. Verses 15-17. Verse 17 holds up to our view the King who we saw in verse 5. In Him there is such a glorious hope and a safe home. Consider what makes Him such a secure hope, worthy of all our trust, in the light of verses 15-16.

In stark contrast to all of us sinful humans, Christ the King is beautiful in His righteousness and always speaks what is right. He can never be corrupted with the treasures of this passing age and will never be involved in our sinful schemes. He cannot even think about evil in any way. Therefore, He alone can ascend the hill of the LORD and dwell safely in the innermost presence of the Most High. The heighest heights welcome Him! Yet, the promise of verse 17 is that if we trust in Him and follow Him, then He will keep us with Him and bring us to Himself.

Isaiah

Study 6 Bible Answers

Isaiah 40:1-14

1. Verse 1-2. Isaiah 39:5-7 announces that though the Assyrian armies have retreated, the Babylonian armies will come to take the people away to exile. How can Isaiah 40:1 follow on from that? What possible comfort could there be in the light of that terrible prophecy?

We do not live forever in this passing age of mortal life. Whether sooner or later we must find a comfort that goes beyond our flesh, a comfort that has everlasting foundations. Whether through Babylonian armies or mortal illness (like Hezekiah), we are flesh that soon withers and dies. The great comfort that gives us true peace and joy in every circumstance is that our sins are paid for; that the LORD has forgiven us; that He is gracious towards us. If we know that He loves us and has a place for us in His resurrection future, then we have real comfort for every trouble.

2. Verse 3. Though the people might be in exile, though they might feel they are in the wilderness or the desert, yet how does this new prophecy give deep comfort and hope? (see Mark 1:1-3).

Right where they were, right where we are, the LORD God comes. Even in the desert exile, the LORD God comes to us bringing us back from exile. While we were yet sinners Christ died for us (Romans 5:8). The road that we prepare is to welcome Him. We want to remove all obstacles from His way when He comes to us. Anything that would hinder His presence or welcome with us must be taken away.

3. Verse 4. Why do valleys need to be raised up and mountains made low? What is this image telling us about the coming of God?

Think of the song that Mary sings while pregnant with Jesus in Luke 1:46-55. She knows that the LORD Jesus Christ within her is coming to bring down the arrogant rulers and lift up the humble; to take from the rich and give to the poor. Think of the words preached by Jesus in Luke 6:20-26. The Church family of Jesus is the place where we share all we have with each other. Think of how the apostolic Church lived this out in Acts 2:44-47.

4. Verse 5. Think about the situation of Isaiah and the ancient Church, surrounded by hostile nations and all kinds of mere 'religion'. How does this verse deal with that?

The world can seem intimidating at times, yet the Way of Jesus leads us out into that world to take His Life and Truth to everyone. Jesus is for the whole world and He comes to set people free whatever their nation or language or religion. Instead of seeing the world as threatening the Church, we need to see it the other way around and realise that the Church is invading the world with the glory of Jesus. Even when we are captured and imprisoned or even killed, the glory of Jesus is able to shine through even in those darkest of places.

5. Verses 6-7. This might sound like an unpromising message to announce to the world, but why is this such an important truth for us all to take to heart? What does this tell us about human glory?

All the way through the book of Isaiah we are shown the vain, empty 'glory' of humanity and the eternal glory of the LORD Jesus Christ. Think of the many ways the LORD, through Isaiah, has shown us the passing, fleeting 'glory' of the nations of the world. Here He cuts right to the basic issue: we are all like grass that lasts such a short time and all our glory is at best like a flower that has a short time to bloom before it fades away. Notice that it is the breath of the LORD that brings death to us all.

6. Verse 8. Is there any hope for mortal human beings? Compare the hope of this verse to the end of verse 5, and consider who the Word of God is.

We were created to have the life of the Eternal Son flowing through us. Cut off from Him we have no life or substance, withering away almost as soon as we appear. Yet, that Eternal Word of God still stands for ever and wonderfully still invites us to return to Him and find in Him that eternal life that He made us for.

7. Verse 9. It is almost as if the prophecy of the coming LORD God has already happened and it is time to preach His arrival. Why would Isaiah do this? Wasn't Christ the LORD still hundreds of years into the future?

Isaiah

Yes, it would be hundreds of years before John the Baptist came as the actual voice preaching the preparation for the work of Christ the LORD, but they did not need to wait that long to trust Him and love Him and worship Him! Christ was already with them, in His pre-incarnate form, as He showed so clearly when He defeated the Assyrian army as the Angel of the LORD.

8. Verse 10. What does this Sovereign LORD bring with Him? (Consider also verses 12-14) Why is this important?

He is the "Sovereign" LORD: He is the one who rules over the world. When Isaiah preached that the best foreign policy is "trust in the LORD", it was proved to be true when the Angel of this Sovereign LORD defeated the Assyrians. The Arm of the LORD rules on His behalf (consider also Isaiah 51:9; 53:1 and John 12:38). A man's arm is where his strength and ability is found: a man with weapons is an "armed" man. The rewards and spoils of His victory are already with Him. It is as if He has already won as soon as He arrives, because His power and ability are so great.

9. Verse 11. How does Christ the LORD use all that power and ability?

Power is so often abused that we tend to think of it as inevitably to do with tyranny. "Power corrupts and absolute power corrupts absolutely" is the common quotation. Yet the almighty Arm of the LORD with a hand that measures the whole universe (verse 12), comes as the Good Shepherd who uses all that mighty power to gently care for His flock, carrying us in His arms. "O what a mystery meekness and majesty, Bow down and worship for this is your God. This is your God!"

(Graham Kendrick, 1986, Thankyou Music)

Study 7   Bible Answers

Isaiah 46:1-13

1. Verses 1-2. If Bel and Nebo were ancient Babylonian gods it seems strange that their worshippers had to carry them (their statues) about on ox drawn carts. Why does Isaiah make such a point about these gods being a burden for weary people?

The Living God does not need any of us to carry Him in any way! In pagan and agnostic philosophies the world is always bigger and older than their gods or systems, therefore they end up having to work for these gods and systems. Any system in which you have to carry around these gods in wagons is shouting out that these gods can do nothing for us. The LORD God knows that we do not even have the strength to save ourselves let alone save these demanding gods.

2. What are the man-made gods in your experience that also require so much support and maintenance? Meditate on entertainment systems that need upgrades and have to be carted away to the tip when they fail or our cars which break down or our houses that need huge amounts of money and effort to support. Are there other things that capture our worship or promise us contentment or fulfilment, things that cost us so much?

We all know that at the end of our lives we will never wish that we had spent more time watching TV or playing games or shopping for 'stuff' or more time decorating our houses. When we die we will take none of these things with us. All these things promise to make us happier, to make us more fulfilled to take away our stress, but in reality they always add to our stress and place demands upon us. If we had nothing but our food, drink and basic clothing, would we not see the simplicity of life so much more clearly and follow the the LORD Jesus Christ with true dependence?

3. Verses 3-4. List the contrasts between the pagan and man-made gods on the one hand and the LORD God on the other. Notice how Isaiah emphasises how the LORD carries His people.

The LORD God has upheld His people since they were conceived, through their childhood and on into old age. He sustains them all the time,

Isaiah

whether they are aware of it or not. In verse 4 when He says "I am He", He is recalling His Name in Exodus 3:14. He is the same: He is and was and will be; the source of all life and existence. The Living God needs no support from us and instead gives us our life and breath. Those pagan 'gods' need to be carried everywhere and require offerings and support from their followers.

4. Verse 5-7. What are the main faults with the man-made idols and the false gods?

The man-made idols are supposed to be earthly 'models' of heavenly beings, but the Living God cannot be compared to anything in the whole creation. The Father, Son and Holy Spirit have a life that is eternally and infinitely beyond everything in the heavens and the earth. The pagan gods require idols or statues that are made from created materials. They can't do anything or go anywhere: they have to be carried around on human shoulders: once the statue is put in place it cannot even move! The gods and idols have nothing to ever say. If they are real and living then why don't they push these statues aside and actually appear and act in real history the way that the LORD Jesus Christ has done? The key problem is listed at the end of verse 7: these gods and idols cannot save; they cannot take away our sin and they cannot give us immortal, resurrection life. They have no life of their own, so they certainly can't give any to us!

5. Verses 8-9. What does the Living God want His people to remember?

When we are unsure of the Father, Son and Spirit today or we are getting carried away by our own sins and desires, we need to remember the living, speaking, active reality of this Living God. Remember the specific real historical actions that He has done in the past. Isaiah may well have been thinking about the real actions and words that the Angel of the LORD accomplished in the Exodus when He took His people to meet the Unseen LORD at Mount Sinai. We can also remember the words He has spoken through the prophets or the actions of the Angel of the LORD here in Isaiah chapter 37. Most of all we can read the four eyewitness accounts of what He did when He was born of the Virgin and lived among us, speaking and acting in normal human history.

6. Verses 10-11. What is the main proof that the LORD God provides that He is the only One who can be trusted?

The LORD's ability to describe and control history is the great proof of His reliabilty and reality in the book of Isaiah. Not only does He explain the past and the present but He also predicts the future in great detail, including the coming of the Babylonian and then the Persian empires. He very specifically describes Cyrus, by name, even though he would not arrive for many decades beyond Isaiah. Of course, the greatest example of this is the way that He constantly and in detail describes the birth, life, death, resurrection, ascension and second coming of the LORD Jesus Christ Himself.

7. Verses 12-13. What is the central promise of the Living God? If we are "far from righteousness" then what is His remedy?

The LORD God brings His own righteousness to us. We have no righteousness of our own and we certainly can't acheive any because every day we fall into sin and fall short of the glory of the Living God. Yet, in coming to us and becoming one of us He brings His own righteousness and lives it out in human life, making it available to us through His death and resurrection. Salvation is His work alone, and all He asks of us is that we receive His saving righteousness with loving trust.

8. Think about conversations we may have had about "the existence of God". Have they been like these words from Isaiah? What should we have done? Did we ever speak about Jesus? Is it possible to speak about the existence of God without talking about Jesus?

Isaiah

Study 8   Bible Answers

Isaiah 51:9-16

1. Verse 9a. This is the first of three calls to "Awake! Awake!": the first is to "the Arm of the LORD"; the second is to Jerusalem (51:17) and the third is to Zion (52:1). What is the difference between these three subjects that are told to "Awake!"? Who is the "Arm of the LORD"?

The Arm of the LORD is the LORD Jesus Christ. If we think of the Living God in terms of a human body then we can see how the Spirit is called the Breath of God, but we also see how God the Son is called the Arm of the LORD, because He is the One who accomplishes the will of His Father. Everything that the One God does is from the Father, through the Son, in the power of the Spirit. So, first, the Arm of the LORD is given a mission from God the Father filled with words of reassurance and wisdom. We can only imagine how precious this Scripture would have been to the LORD Jesus as He grew up as a human boy: it must have almost felt as if He were back in the glory of heaven listening to His Father instructing Him. The second Awake (51:17) is to the earthly city of Jerusalem that has been afflicted with so much sin and punishment, reassuring her that the LORD will take the cup of wrath from her. The third Awake (52:1) is to the heavenly Jerusalem, Zion herself, speaking of the purity and safety and salvation that belong to her.

2. Verses 9-10. The whole section is addressed to "the Arm of the LORD", so what did He do in "generations of old"? What incident from "days gone by" is being remembered here? Who is Rahab? (See Isaiah 30:7).

Rahab is another name for Egypt, so the LORD is reminding them of the time when He rescued them from Egypt in the Exodus. He made a dry road through the Red Sea, showing His awesome power over the sea.

3. Verse 11. It is as if the people of Judah are already in exile even though the Babylonian exile was still decades into the future. What is the deeper 'exile' that Isaiah is speaking of here? What is the final hope that he is holding up for the Church in every age?

In the deepest sense the whole human race (even the entire creation itself) has been in exile since Genesis chapter 3 when Adam and Evil joined the devil in beginning the creation's sinful rebellion. Right from that original sin the world has been in exile from the Living God, driven out of His presence. Alienated from the life of God the little life we have slips away from us until we decay away into death and dust, but even more seriously this corruption of death rots away in our hearts and minds long before it takes our bodies. Nevertheless, this exile ends in the LORD Jesus Christ: we will return into Zion, the City of God, and one day all sorrow and sighing will flee away as the earth is filled with the knowledge of the LORD God Almighty.

4. Verse 12-13a. Why is it so important to spend time every day thinking about "Our Father in heaven"? Why did Jesus, the Arm of the LORD, have to keep that in mind as He faced His great work on earth?

God the Creator, the Heavenly Father, is still on the throne of all creation, even though the world may have fallen into exile. We pray that His will be done "on earth" just as it is done "in heaven". When we are surrounded by the rebellion of sinful humanity, in all its many forms but especially in the form of tyranny and persecution, we need to always remember our Heavenly Father who stretched out all the millions of galaxies and established the incredible wonder of life on earth. What are any mortal human beings, no matter how oppressive or arrogant, compared to Him?

5. Verse 13. When we are surrounded by all the empires, tyrannies and ideologies of this passing age, how can we be free from fear or "constant terror"?

The only way to be free of fear is to fear the LORD God Himself. When the fear of the LORD grips our hearts and minds, then it is peace and love that flood our hearts rather than "constant terror". So many of us live in constant terror of disease or trouble, yet the LORD Jesus Christ Himself told us never to worry, but to trust our Father in heaven who cares for us. Until we can genuinely let go of all our fears and trust Him to care for us, we can never escape our fears.

6. Verse 14. We can easily fall into the view that the sufferings and troubles of this mortal life as the end of the story, as if they had the

Isaiah

final word. What is the Biblical remedy for this? Why did this comfort have special power for the Arm of the LORD in His great work?

If we look at life and death from the perspective of our mortal flesh then we see only darkness and despair when the evil powers of this age triumph, especially if we are their victims. What hope can there be for justice or for the future of God's family if evil seems to triumph? We need to always remind ourselves of that final Great Day of Resurrection. Jesus had to keep His eyes fixed on the joy set before Him in order to endure the shame of the Cross and death. He had to constantly trust His Father to vindicate Him in His resurrection and the new creation of all things.

7. Verse 15. Why is it so important to know that the LORD God has power over the sea?

The sea is the constant symbol of chaos and rebellion throughout the Bible. We see this in verses 9-10 as the LORD declares His victory over Egypt at the Red Sea. We need to know that when the ocean of chaos seems to overwhelm us that even that is under the control of the Heavenly Father on the throne of heaven.

8. Verse 16. The final words are specially spoken to the Arm of the LORD by His Father in heaven, but they also include Zion, the Church of the Living God – "You are my people". What is the great comfort of this verse?

The Creator who made the heavens and the earth has planned the future of the Church before everything else. Before the foundation of the universe He elected the Church in His Eternal Son Jesus Christ. The stability of the heavens and the earth is a testament to the stability of His promise to Zion, His Church: "You are my people". This great purpose of all things for the Church is what drove God the Son to be born as One of us, to live our life and die our death. He has done everything so that the Church will be His Bride forever and ever. This promise has deeper foundations than the universe itself.

Study 9 Bible Answers

Isaiah 57:11-21

1. Verse 11. What were the fears and worries that occupied the hearts and minds of the ancient Church in Isaiah's day? What are the fears and worries that have the same effect on the Church today?

Judah and Jerusalem were completely paralysed by their fear of the invading armies of Assyria and then Babylon. Clearly the people couldn't stop imagining the terrible suffering if soldiers came to brutally kill them, or abuse them, taking their homes, children and possessions. It is a very powerful fear and it would be hard to see beyond this fear. Today many people are gripped by their fear of health problems, financial disaster, family tragedy or even the fear of losing their capactizes as they grow older. Again, all these are real and powerful fears, so we need to follow the Way of the LORD Jesus Christ with all our heart to escape such fears.

2. Verse 11b. Why do we find it so hard to walk by faith and not by sight? If we do not see or hear the LORD God almost all the time, why do we so quickly stop trusting Him?

The very heart and centre of sin is doubt. Adam and Eve fell into sin because they would not trust the LORD in the original Garden. We might imagine that if only we had a particular experience or sight or sound then we would be free from doubt forever, but that is never the case. We will always begin to doubt whatever we saw or heard unless we fundamentally trust the LORD Jesus Christ. As the Creator and Sustainer of all things, He is Himself the basic guarantee of the reality and truthfulness of experience itself! He even tells us to taste and see that the LORD is good (Psalm 34:8), but unless we ask and seek with genuine trust we will never really taste and we will never truly see. If the scientist refuses to trust her observations or the reality of the world around her then she can never make any progress. The first step of knowledge must always be that basic step of trust as we are genuinely open to reality. The corruption of sin in our hearts and minds always turns us in on ourselves in a selfish and narrow prison that is always looking for signs. Please take time to read Matthew 12:38-45.

Isaiah

3. Verse 12. Why does the LORD point at "your righteousness and your works"?

The danger is that instead of taking refuge in Him so that we can taste and see His goodness we take refuge in whatever righteousness or works we feel are of value. This may range from religious zeal or family heritage, common decency to self-improvement discipline; yet, none of these things will benefit us in the presence of the Living God. All these things are worthless if we are going to genuinely share His eternal life.

4. Verse 13. Compare the refuge offered by the idols with the refuge offered by the LORD Jesus Christ?

Those idols who need to be carried around, who cannot move or speak, or those gods who never actually appear in human history, cannot even survive a strong wind. The idols might be set up but a good gust of wind will blow them over! If we tried to take refuge behind them we might be crushed as they toppled over! By contrast the Eternal and Majestic God offers Himself as a true refuge for His people and whoever finds a never failing refuge in Him will not only inherit the earth itself but also the highest heaven with the mountain of God Himself, the City of Zion. Consider Psalm 2:12 and Psapm 5:11-12 on the theme of taking refuge in Christ the LORD.

5. Verse 14. Why does the LORD command this obstacle-free road to be built?

This again emphasises the way that the Living God comes to serve His people, making life easier for them taking burdens off them. The idols and gods and the religious systems add burdens, rules and obstacles, but the real and Living God is concerned only to remove the obstacles and clear the road.

6. Verse 15. How can the Living God live both in the highest heaven and also in the lowliest heart? What does this tell us about the nature and glory of the Father, Son and Holy Spirit?

First, Jesus on earth told us to daily think of "our Father in heaven" and He also promised that God the Holy Spirit would come and dwell with us. When we have a deep and rich understanding of the Trinity we can see how the One Living God has within Himself not only that high

transcendence of the Father and the mediation of the Son but also the indwelling and immanence of the Holy Spirit.

Second, this Living God shows His greatest glory not by standing far off in His own self-absorbed majesty, but by His self-sacrificial redemption of all those who love and trust Him. Nothing thrills us so much as the way He takes "no hopers" like us and gives us the hope of sharing His own eternal life as His own family!

7. Verse 16-18. What do we learn here about the anger of the Living God? How does His anger compare to human anger?

The anger of the Living God is always under His control. Yes, it is real and powerful so that we dare not dismiss it as mere metaphor, but it does not control Him as the passions of the ancient Greek and Roman gods controlled them. Even when He feels rage at the selfish evil that we do, He does not lash out or lose His temper. His gospel purposes and love always have the final word over the life of His Church.

8. Verses 19-21. In Jeremiah 6:14 the false prophets preach "peace, peace" when there is no peace. How does their false message compare to the preaching of the LORD Himself? Is it fair to say that the message of "peace, peace" must be preached to the Lord's people rather than to the wicked?

The LORD preaches "peace, peace" to His people, to the Church that finds her refuge in Him. To the Church, who may so often feel that everything around her and within is far from peaceful, He lovingly, constantly, profoundly preaches eternal peace to her, a peace beyond understanding that the world can never give. Yet, He will never give this peace and rest to the wicked. They have no future at all with Him. The false prophets insist on preaching this "peace, peace" to the wicked!

9. One of the great challenges that many are facing today is how to live in loving friendship with people who either ignore, reject or misunderstand the Way of Jesus. Many of our friends, families and neighbours follow belief systems that are committed to other gods or philosophies, and have a very different view of Jesus. What would Isaiah have thought of the idea that as long as people are sincere or open to love in whatever beliefs they have the LORD God might just welcome them into the new creation anyway?

Isaiah

Isaiah has shown us very clearly and profoundly that the LORD God doesn't simply want people to live in some kind of 'eternal paradise'. The whole point of everything He has done from creation and on into that new creation future, at the cost of His own suffering and blood on the Cross, is so that He can be personally married to His Church in the deepest bonds of love. The Living God wants us: our hearts and minds given with free hearts that love Him and trust Him now and forever. The point of salvation is to set us free from all the religion, systems, blindness and idolatry that grips us in our sinful mess. If people will not ask or seek or knock; if they will not trust Him but stay in their own "righteousness and works" (57:12) then there will be no atonement for them. Why does the LORD God constantly and so passionately plead with His Church and the whole world to come to Him in repentance and faith if it was not absolutely essential that we really do that? Why would He have gone to the extremities of Isaiah 52:13-53:12 if there was any other way?

Study 10 Bible Answers

Isaiah 62:1-63:6

1. Verse 1. This is one of the most emotionally intense parts of the whole Bible as we see the LORD God as the loving husband of His new bride (62:4-5) but also as He comes in saving judgment against the world (63:1-6). So, what is the great passion that motivates the great redemption plans of the Living God?

Everything is for the sake of Zion, the Church, His great family and Body (Ephesians 1:22-23). The reason for the whole creation was that the glory of Christ might be shared and expressed through His Church for endless ages. Until His righteousness shines through her "like the dawn" He will keep working and speaking.

2. Verses 2-3. With all the kings of the earth looking to the Great King, where does His Church, fit in this picture?

The nations are drawn to the LORD by looking to the shining righteousness of the Church. Jesus Himself said "let your light shine before men, that they may see your good deeds and praise your Father in heaven" (Matthew 5:16). It is as if the LORD reigns through the royal diadem or crown that is the Church. It is beyond our imagination to grasp how the Eternal and Infinite God is determined to share His life with His people for all eternity, literally exercising His reign through us.

3. Verses 4-5. Verse 2 mentioned a new name and now we learn what it is: Hephzibah (*my delight is in her*); and the name of the land is Beulah (*married*). Thinking about the beginning and end of the Bible, how do these verses take us to the very heart of the meaning of the universe itself?

When Paul comments on Genesis 2:24 in Ephesians 5:22-32 he reminds us that the original creation of Adam and Eve always had in view that bigger picture of Christ and His Church. The goal of the whole creation is for the Church to be married to the LORD God Himself. Jesus Himself tells us that the whole creation is heading to a wedding celebration – Matthew 25:1-13 and in Revelation 19:7-10 and Revelation 21:1-5 we see that happening.

Isaiah

4. Verses 6-7. How do these verses connect to the Lord's Prayer — "may your kingdom come and your will be done on earth as in heaven"?

The LORD is telling His people to constantly pray for this great conclusion to history. We should be just as eager as He is to strain towards that final day of Justice, that divine wedding day when everything will be put right. Even now we do all we can to make the kingdom of God a reality while we wait for that day: "give yourselves no rest and give Him no rest"!

5. Verses 8-9. Looking ahead to that time when the City of God is established in the new creation, compare these verses with the description of the resurrection future in 65:21-22.

It is important to see how tangible and real the new creation hope is in the Bible. In popular culture and philosophical abstractions, the only hope is some 'ghostly' existence in 'heaven' or some vague hope of 'something better than we can imagine'. However, the Bible shows us the real hope that we can genuinely hold onto: this world will be utterly renewed and all the very good things that the LORD God created will be enjoyed as they were always supposed to be.

6. Verses 10-12. Why would a message about "the Daughter of Zion" be proclaimed to the ends of the earth?

All through Isaiah we have seen how the mission of the Church is to bring in and spread out among all the nations of the world. In verse 10 the road is prepared for all the LORD's people, but a banner is raised up to summon all the nations to join in with His people on this highway to Zion. The LORD God is coming with this glorious future already accomplished: this is not a new creation that we have to acheive with our own feeble efforts — and this is for the whole world. His Holy People are Redeemed people, saved out of all the nations of the world. Zion is "Sought After", "No Longer Deserted" because the international crowds fill her streets.

7. Verses 1-3. Throughout the book of Isaiah we have often seen how the Holy One of Israel is all alone in His righteousness and opposition to evil, but here that fact strikes home with a vivid

intensity. Why has the reality of the winepress of God's wrath been seen as such good news by millions of people down through history?

We yearn for that wonderful new creation future, but for that to happen the world needs to be judged and cleaned out. All through this passing age the oppressors and tyrants have crushed their victims under their feet; the empires have killed and plundered as they will; the rich have lived at the expense of the poor. The LORD God must first set all these things right and force the wicked to face up to what they have done. Part of giving His oppressed people rest is showing them that He cared for them even when they were suffering. The victims of the world long for justice, a justice that is rarely even glimpsed in this dark age. Yet, on that day, real, balanced justice will be done and the great Divine hero will stand up for goodness and truth once and for all.

8. Verses 4-6. What is the great motivation of Christ the LORD in His lonely work?

For the joy of the new creation, for His great love for His bride, Christ will judge the world and put everything right, no matter how messy or difficult that work will be. He knows that we can never do that work for Him: we are too involved and infected by the darkness and sin of this old world. Vengeance and anger are always mixed up with selfishness and sin in our own hearts and minds, so Christ the LORD must do this work alone, sustained by His own righteous anger against all that is wrong. That cup of wrath that He personally drank for the whole world, will now be forced on those who refused to shelter in Him. Praise God that Jesus does this work alone and praise God that He does it out of love for His Church.

Isaiah

Appendix 1

List of Isaiah references found in the New Testament

Isaiah Reference	New Testament Location
1:9	Romans 9:29
6:9	Matthew 13:14; Mark 4:12; Luke 8:10; John 12:39; Acts 28:25
7:14	Matthew 1:23
8:12	1 Peter 3:14
8:14	Romans 9:33; 1 Peter 2:8
8:17-18	Hebrews 2:13
9:1	Matthew 4:15
9:6	Matthew 1:23
10:22	Romans 9:27
11:5	Ephesians 6:14
11:10	Romans 15:12
22:13	1 Corinthians 15:32
22:22	Revelation 3:7
25:8	1 Corinthians 15:54
27:9	Romans 11:26
28:11	1 Corinthians 14:21
28:16	Romans 9:33; 10:11; 1 Peter 2:6
29:10	Romans 11:8
29:13	Matthew 15:7; Mark 7:6
29:14	1 Corinthians 1:19
29:16	Romans 9:19-21
40:3	Matthew 3:3; Mark 1:2; Luke 3:4; John 1:23
40:6	1 Peter 1:25
40:13	Romans 11:34

Isaiah Reference	New Testament Location
42:1	Matthew 12:18
42:4	Romans 15:12
42:6	Luke 2:32
45:23	Romans 14:11
49:6	Luke 2:32; Acts 13:47
49:8	2 Corinthians 6:2
52:5	Romans 2:24
52:7	Romans 10:15
52:11	2 Corinthians 6:17
52:15	Romans 15:21
53:1	John 12:38; Romans 10:16
53:4	Matthew 8:17
53:7	Acts 8:32
53:9	1 Peter 2:22
53:12	Mark 15:28; Luke 22:37
54:1	Galatians 4:27
54:13	John 6:45
55:3	Acts 13:34
56:7	Matthew 21:13; Mark 11:17; Luke 19:46
59:7-8	Romans 3:15-17
59:17	Ephesians 6:14-17
59:20	Romans 11:26
61:1	Luke 4:17
64:4	1 Corinthians 2:9
65:1-2	Romans 10:20-21
66:1	Acts 7:48
66:24	Mark 9:48

Isaiah

Appendix 2

Israel and Judah at the time of Isaiah